GYŐZŐ MARGÓCZI

THE WAY FEELINGS CONTROL OUR MIND

Budapest, Hungary
2016

Translation made ont the basis of
Margóczi Győző: Szavak

Copyright © Margóczi Győző, 2015
English translation: Gábor Szkórits-Tala
Copy editor: Patricia Hughes

ISBN 978-963-12-5327-6

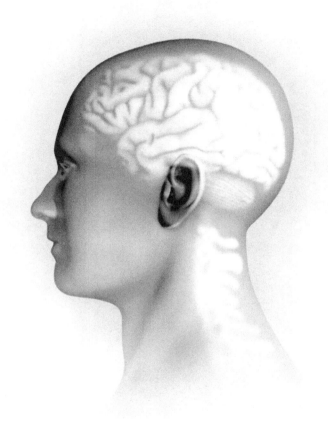

WORDS

CONTENTS

INTRODUCTION

Humankind is in trouble, deep trouble.

If we look at the bright side of the coin, we people have achieved incredible things. We open year-round indoor ski tracks in the hottest desert. We build skyscrapers and luxury hotels, equipped with all conceivable amenities, at an incredible speed. The wonders of electronics are present in every facet of our lives. We investigate the secrets of the structure of matter with our huge and incredibly complex particle accelerators. We are experienced users of nuclear energy. We create all kinds of new synthetic compounds. Biologists explore the operation of the human organism to ever greater degrees. We have conquered the depths of the oceans. We have left the Solar System and are aiming at reaching other planets. These things could only be achieved because we have amassed enormous amounts of technical knowledge.

And what is the case with the darker side of the coin? After deploying two atomic bombs, we still have huge arsenals of nuclear weapons facing each other. Unstable statelets are persistently trying to make their own nuclear weapons. Secret chemical and biological weapons are aimed at targets in the depths of hidden storage sites. Despite the millions killed in the first and second World Wars, since then more people have been killed in local conflicts than in World War II. There are bloody civil wars everywhere, not only in Africa, Asia or South America but also in the heart of Europe: just think of the Yugoslav Wars. You see airliners blown up, cars bombed, schoolchildren taken hostage and killed, riots, unrest, religious and ethnic hatred everywhere. We are staggering from one economic crisis to another. We are polluting our environment, soil and water. We are destroying the living world, the flora and fauna of our planet. Millions of people are starving and living in poverty. Billions of people are living hopeless lives. And the problems do not only affect undeveloped regions! Quite a number of people live under subsistence level in Europe and North America. The majority of humankind lives in both physical and mental poverty. According to the findings of a research group, more than one quarter of Europe's population suffers from some kind of mental illness.

During the daily grind we try not to think of these dreadful facts but our dark present will be followed by an even darker future. I personally think that while humankind has achieved great things in the sciences, it has hardly moved at all in human studies. You may ask why. What's the reason? And where is the way out? Where shall we start? This book is intended to give an answer to some of these rather difficult questions.

The author

STRANGE BUT NO ONE SEEMS TO NOTICE

If an actor in any country in the world walked into the local aeroplane design institute and said he wanted to design passenger aeroplanes just because he felt like it, they would ask him: "But, man do you have a degree in physics, electrical engineering or mechanical engineering? How can you imagine that you would be able to be involved in the design of something on whose safety the lives of hundreds of people depend? Are you insane? Don't you understand? This is an enormous responsibility!"

I guess each and every one of my readers agrees and nods diligently. A man who is not an expert of a field the control of which people's lives depend on should stay away from the steering wheel and should not interfere with things he does not understand!

After all this, the question is rightly raised: Why was an actor appointed the President of the United States of America? Didn't the fate of the 300 million people living in the US matter, or the fate of all the billions in the world US has influence over?

Yes I know, many of you are now thinking that the president does not make his decisions alone, hundreds of scientists work in the preparation of his decisions. My answer to that is: this is then exactly like an aeroplane design institute where scientists work everywhere but the chief constructor is still an actor. I personally would not really like to fly in an aeroplane like that.

Have you, dear reader, ever considered the fact that while scientists do everything in the field of technology, is not scientists but dilettante politicians that have all the power in the most complicated system, our society? And anyone can be a politician if they get elected! Imagine the following dialogue in the aeroplane design institute we mentioned above: "I think we should trust Joe with designing the wings. I think Joe is a nice guy. The neighbour of the younger brother of my wife's niece meets him sometimes in the street and he always greets her very politely. And he's nice anyway because he has a moustache. True, he didn't finish high school (and indeed had to repeat his first and second years several times)." Would you, dear reader, be ready to fly in a plane with wings designed by Joe?

This, after all, is roughly the way we elect our politicians. And we didn't even mention the human and psychological fitness of those politicians! How many selfish and corrupt politicians are in positions of power? Did any psychologist ever examine whether they were suitable for the position in mental moral or psychological terms before they took up their position? If I want to have a gun licence, I must obtain millions of documents and I also need to visit a psychologist who tells me I am not nuts and I will not slaughter innocent people with my single pistol. "This is perfectly normal and in order" my dear reader may think. You cannot give a gun to just anybody. But has a psychologist ever examined the president of any country to discover what he is going to use the thousands of atomic bombs, tens of thousands of tanks and aeroplanes, and millions of guns at his disposal for? Did any psychologist ever examine the mental state of Hitler before he became the Chancellor of the Reich? It is not that funny anymore, is it?

And then there is the word 'democracy'. If an aeroplane design institute was not a terrible, disgusting, anti-democratic institution, then its employees could decide with voting if they want to make an aeroplane of aluminium or concrete, for example, and, after working hours, they could also vote on whether the Earth should orbit around the Sun or the other way round.

You cannot vote about whether an aeroplane should be built of aluminium or enforced concrete! Or you can but you should not be surprised if the result does not fly. We should understand that the diverse processes of the world around us are regulated by strict laws and these processes will not adapt to democracy, to votes or to our wishes for that matter.

And people understand it all right... as long as it's about the issues of technology, chemistry or biology. But the moment we start to talk about human life, these laws seem to lose their power. But they only lose their power in people's minds, not in reality! In reality it is life that slaps us in the face and we just stand there baffled.

When the existence and welfare of humankind are at stake, we must pay attention to the laws of our world and scientists must control society and not the attempted politicians or the mighty dwarfs who supply them with money. Because, if we allow ourselves the luxury of not doing so, we will have to face serious negative consequences.

You may now think that all we have to do is to discover

the laws of our society and to adapt to them. And it is indeed the case. However, these things tend to work only with great difficulty for some reason. Something or somebody seems to hinder the process. But what is the reason why these processes go so slowly?

1.

THE STARTING POINT

In order to better understand the current status quo I am suggesting that we draw a parallel between an aeroplane and society, as well as between a pilot and a politician. Let us start with the aeroplane. Although we would have the same result with any of the parts of the aeroplane, for the sake of clarity, I recommend using the thrust lever. I think it's a familiar sight for all of us from action movies, when the pilot, with a severe and determined look on his face, pushes the thrust lever ahead and the aircraft suddenly gains momentum.

But what do we know about the thrust lever? The answer is very simple: everything. We know the precise operation mechanism of the thrust lever. We know what parts the thrust lever is connected to and we also know what other parts the parts connected to the thrust lever are connected to and what other parts these new parts are connected to. That is, we know each and every part (linkages, levers, arms, shell bearings, roller bearings etc.) between the thrust lever and the engine. But it's not only the parts that we know, we also know exactly how they work. We know that the axis of rotation of the thrust lever is connected to the body of the aeroplane with small roller bearings, that the rocker connected to the thrust lever to transform the circular movement of the thrust lever to linear movement is connected to the thrust lever with a small peg and that this peg is kept in place with a spring-type O ring. And, in addition to knowing the way the parts are connected, we also know the exact parameters of the entire operation mechanism. We can calculate, if the pilot pushes the thrust lever ahead with a certain force (F1) and speed (V1), at what speed (V2) the rocker will move and what force (F2) will be applied on it and, eventually, how much this small movement will increase the thrust of the engine. In order to be able to design such a complicated and serviceable mechanism, the engineers had to design every single part to very high tolerances. And the important word in this sentence is design because learning and understanding everything about something is not as complicated as designing the same thing and then creating it in reality. The conditions of existence:

But for the time being, let's stick to learning and understanding. What do we know about the throttle lever? To what degree do we know it? Completely, for all practical reasons. We know its geometrical shape, dimensions, physical characteristics (mass, specific weight, thermal expansion coefficient, electrical conductivity, tensile strength, roughness, magnetic permeability, etc.), what kind of alloy it is made of, what materials the alloy contains and what the physical characteristics of these materials are, right down to the level of the atoms (we only have controversial ideas about the subatomic level). When the pilot (with a determined look on his face) decides to increase the flying speed of the aeroplane, he is practically aware of the entire process of acceleration. He can, if he likes, follow the whole process of acceleration in his thoughts.

Now let us have a politician sit in the cockpit of the country and ask him to 'accelerate'. That is where problems begin. The politician will scratch his head and exclaim: "Oh, my God! Which one is the thrust lever here?" In order to help him, we point to lever whose label says 'tax reduction'. The label 'tax reduction' is a concept. It does not denote a concrete, tangible object like 'thrust lever', for example, which is a relatively easily definable object both in terms of its physical characteristics and in terms of the role it plays in the system. The meaning of the words 'tax reduction' is clear for everyone. We all know that in the case of a tax reduction, we will have to pay less money to the government and we will have more money to spend on whatever we want. What is there not to understand? It is perfectly clear. Or is it?

What happens if we start to analyse these words further? What is 'tax'? What is 'reduction'? What is 'money'? What is 'pay'? What is 'government'? What is 'no'? What is 'spend'? What is 'want'? Oh, come on! Everyone knows what these words and concepts mean. Are you sure? Let us try to define the word 'tax' that is so clear to everyone. If you check the word 'tax' on the Internet, you will find something like this: "Tax is a regular (or sometimes extraordinary) material – usually financial – contribution private or legal persons pay to a superior power." This is a well-phrased easy to understand definition. Or is it? Because, what is a 'private person'? What is a 'legal person'? What is 'superior'? What is 'power'? What is 'regular'? What is 'contribution'?

I went to a mathematics and physics class at the Diósgyőr high school in Hungary where Mr Lajos Bagoly tried to knock the signs of physics into our head, sometimes literally. He was a very strict guy, but we did learn physics. Thank you, teacher! We always had to express ourselves very accurately. If a student had tried to answer a question like this: "Listen, teacher, the atom is a what-do-you-call-it that consists of those little thingies which are made up of even smaller thingummies that are then made up of stuff.", he would have been given such a slap in the face that his head would have fallen off.

When we are trying to define concepts in the field of hu-

21

man studies, we often do nothing more than the fictitious student in the paragraph above: we are trying to define undefined words with other undefined words. It is an interesting phenomenon that everyone notices such a thing in the field of sciences and no one notices it in the field of human studies.

Of course we can use undefined concepts when talking about the thrust lever. For example: "The thrust lever regulates the amount of fuel that enters the engine through a linkage." This is all very nice and true but try to implement the regulation of the fuel supply of an engine on the basis of this one sentence! It will never work. Unless… Unless you define these words, and therefore the entire process, to the deepest possible depth.

In human studies, people often use words such as freedom, democracy, values, truth, reason, emotions, spirit, perfection, etc. and they do it without actually knowing the meaning of all these words. Moreover, they are firmly convinced that they do indeed know the meaning of the words they are using. Philosophers remind me of a builder whose task it is to build a castle. The builder will put the required elements of the building together with the utmost possible care so they fit most closely. He will do it using the strictest rules of logic so that the building blocks overlap nicely in order to provide a solid structure. He will join partition walls to main walls to further increase the stability of the building. Apparently, everything is in perfect order. But… Yet again, another annoying 'but'. The problem is that our fictitious builder does not examine the building blocks he is using and he does not notice that some of the blocks are made of ice and not baked clay or stone. And if the weather starts to warm up, the beautiful castle built with perfect logic will collapse. You cannot build a castle of substandard building blocks. And the building blocks of human thinking are words. Therefore we cannot take a single step without examining the words themselves.

One badly defined, substandard word, and our apparently bright and brilliant train of thought immediately collapses. Just as an aeroplane may crash because of one badly defined, incorrectly designed part. It is interesting to see that while we take it for granted that before building an aeroplane, we thoroughly examine each and every part, no one seems to notice that when creating systems of theories that will influence the life of millions we kindly disregard the examination of the words.

2.

WHAT IS A WORD?

Although I am using words –you cannot write a book without words – to find out what a 'word' is, in order not to repeat the mistakes of our predecessors, I will try to avoid defining undefined concepts with other undefined concepts. I am going to use words because I cannot do otherwise but I am asking the dear reader not to concentrate on the meaning of those words but, please, think of words as a painter does of her easel that does not explain the landscape you see, only depicts it. In order to prevent hairsplitting, I am deliberately going to use the first person singular, that is, I am going to write down everything in the first person singular and I am asking the reader to interpret everything I write in the first person singular, too, just as if you yourself saw, felt, did or thought it. Well, let us start then…

I am sitting here with this book in my hand and reading. If I raise my head, I see the world around me. Now I am raising my hand and turning it to the light. I see that the side of my hand towards the light is brighter, whereas the other side is darker: I see that my environment has an impact on me. If I now look down at the floor, I notice the shadow of my hand: I see that I also have an impact on my environment. Now

I look up to the sky and I see a rainbow. I am recalling in my memory what I learnt about light. Light is nothing else but the range of electromagnetic radiation I, as a human being, can see. Every wavelength has its own colour. Does the programme of the Hungarian radio channel M1 have a colour? Does BBC World News have a colour? Or does x-ray radiation have one? No. Electromagnetic radiation does not have a colour in itself. Colour is something that only exists in me, a human being; something that is only created when a narrow spectrum of electromagnetic radiation interacts with my nervous system. So I cannot say the sky is blue or the grass is green, I can only say I see the sky as blue and the grass as green. This form of this beautiful world only exists in me, a human being.

I suddenly hear a blackbird singing. Such a beautiful sound! Recalling what I learnt about sound, sound is nothing else but the range of the vibration of the air that has an impact on my nervous system. The vibration of the air is not yet a sound, it is only the dance or movement of the gas molecules which constitute the air. This dance of molecules is only transformed to sound when it interacts with my nervous system through my eardrum and the structures of my middle and internal ear.

So I cannot say the blackbird was emitting a sound, I can only say I perceive the vibration of the air generated by the blackbird as a birdsong. The sound of the blackbird, this beautiful music, actually only exists in me. Outside of me, this is only the silent dance of the molecules of the ocean of air.

I reach into my pocket and produce an apple. I can taste the flavour of the apple if I bite into it and my saliva can dissolve materials from the apple that can interact with my nervous system. I bite into the apple and feel it has a slightly sour taste. As a matter of fact, the apple does not have a taste; the apple only contains a mass of complex chemical molecules. So, in fact, I cannot say my apple has a slightly sour taste, the only thing I can say is if I interact with the apple, the feeling of a sour taste is generated in my body. The feeling of the taste only exists in me and not in the apple. And I could go on listing similar examples: the case is the same with smells and temperature.

What is the mistake humankind commits? What is the thing the great thinkers of the past did not notice? They did not differentiate between the world they experienced and the world around them. They cherished the thought that there is an absolute real world. But the world I experience is only one side of the world. The world has many many sides, just as many as there are people examining it or interacting with it. There is no single and absolute world. The world is relative. What this world looks like depends on who is looking at it, who is examining it and who is involved in what interaction with it?

If a Martian is watching the world, the world the Martian sees will not be the same world I see because she will have different interactions with the world around her. She may perceive different ranges of light, and what I experience as the colour red, she may perceive as the colour blue. The vibrations of her environment will generate different feelings in her. She may not be able to perceive the vibration of gases at all, i.e. she may not hear: sounds may not exist for her. She may enter into different interactions with gases, vapours and various compounds than I do. So, different feelings of smell and taste are generated in her, if at all. And so on and so forth.

The world is nothing else but an immense mass of interactions, where the result of interactions depends on what is interacting with what. At least two participants are needed for each and every interaction. In my case, it is my nervous system and the world around me. In order to have an accurate picture of these interactions, it makes sense to examine them from multiple aspects.

For an external observer, sound is the specific pattern of excitement induced in my nervous system by the specific movement of gas molecules of the air around me. From my point of view, sound is the feeling of sound triggered by the specific movements of the gas molecules of the air around me. (I am asking my dear reader to accept the statement that sounds are feelings without any reasoning for the moment) Sounds, and therefore words, cannot exist outside me. It is only the vibration of the gas molecules of the air that exists outside me.

The simplest way to demonstrate the difference between the internal and the external point of view is to imagine an engineer who is sitting in front of a radio receiver examining the signals in every part of the radio receiver with a complicated oscilloscope but who cannot hear anything of the radio programme because someone else is wearing the headphones. The engineer, who represents the point of view of the external observer, will find that the radio waves make the electrons move and the electrons induce voltage in other parts of the device through a coil and the amplified flow of electrons enters a coil which moves a magnet to which a plastic sheet is attached that is moving the air. The engineer is fully aware of the entire process but does not hear the broadcast. And the person who is sitting in the other room listening to the programme represents the internal point of view. He is not aware of the process taking place within the radio but he hears the programme and a feeling of sound is generated in him.

For the external observer, a word is nothing else but a pattern of nervous excitement – triggered in a person by a specific vibration of the air created by another person – that is assigned to another pattern of nervous excitement created in the person as a result of the electromagnetic radiation, the chemical compounds and the pressure of the external world, the vibration of the gas molecules that constitute the air and the impact that changes the kinetic energy of the surface of the skin or as a result of internal changes.

From my point of view, a word is a specific series of feelings of sound triggered in me by another person, which I associate with the feelings of sight, hearing, smell, taste, touch, and other feelings.

How does the other person come into the picture? It is simple. I do not usually invent words, instead, I hear them for the first time from my environment, from another person and I learn them from him or her (let us now kindly disregard the special case where I invent a word and I do not utter it unless I am certain that no one else can hear it). I learn these series of feelings of sound representing words from other persons and I also learn from other persons which other feelings I should associate these feelings with. To put it more simply, I learn both the sounds of the words and the phenomena related to them from other persons.

Extinct languages no longer spoken by anyone also prove this theory. The remainders of these languages are represented only by signs carved in stones or written on old rolls of parchment. However, these signs are not words but only dents in a block of stone or patches of paint on a broken roll of parchment, nothing else. These are not words because I do not know how to pronounce them, i.e. what kinds of series of feelings of sound belong to them and I do not know either which phenomena of the world I know these signs are associated with. And there is no person who could teach me that.

The situation is slightly better in the case of foreign languages. A word uttered in a language that is foreign to me is not a word for me, only a series of feelings of sound. It only becomes a word when I already know which phenomenon to attach the given series of feelings of sound to. Naturally, I can recall series of feelings of sound representing words also from my memory. In these cases, I perceive these words as 'internal sounds'.

I will now take a common definition of words: "word is the smallest meaningful unit of a language". This is a short, concise, effective and easy to understand statement. It is so precise, it is almost beautiful. The usual problems start to occur when I begin to analyse this definition. What is language? What is meaning? And so on. These are complex, difficult to define concepts. What is the situation with my definition? It is pretty long: you may need to re-read it several times in order to put the picture together accurately but if I start to ask questions about the words in it, I can get clear and in-depth answers, just like in the case of our example about the thrust lever. What is nervous excitement? I can ask a biologist who will have me sit down in front of the microscope and tell me everything about nerve cells, their materials, construction and operation. He will tell me exactly when a nerve cell is in a state of excitement and what the characteristics of such a state are.

So far, so good. Now I know what a word is but it makes sense to shed light on some of its characteristics.

3.

BEING ACCURATE

When, as a result of my interactions with the external world, I see something or various feelings are generated in me, how accurately do these images and feelings reflect reality? Rather inaccurately. My interactions with the environment that do not enter into interactions with my nervous system remain unnoticed by me. I do not see the ultraviolet radiation of the sun, for instance, so I do not get to know of it, although this interaction does exist because, after over-exposure to it, in a couple of days my skin peels off. Similarly, I do not see the radiations in the infrared range emitted by different objects, however, they also exist. So, when I associate a series of feelings of sound with a phenomenon, I associate this series of feelings of sound with a rather inaccurately defined thing.

Beware! I do not assign the series of feelings of sound to the phenomenon existing in the external world but to the pattern of nervous excitement induced in me in connection with the given phenomenon! The phenomenon of the external world – although it exists independently from me – only appears to me through the pattern of nervous excitement resulting from my interaction with this phenomenon. To put it more simply, I do not associate the series of feelings of sound with the rose itself but with the image of the rose appearing in me.

As a matter of fact, a rose is much more than what I can see of it (the resolution of my eyes does not make it possible for me to see all the details: I cannot see the infrared or other radiations leaving the rose or just being absorbed by it, neither can I see the water molecules vaporising from it etc.) and the rose is not red, as I see it, at all in reality (the colour red only exists in me).

On the other hand, the situation is not too rosy with the series of feelings of sound that I assign to a given phenomenon, since the series of sounds are highly inaccurate things, no matter which aspect I am examining them from. From the point of view of an external observer, I cannot vibrate the molecules of the gases that form the air in exactly the same way. To put it more simply but less accurately, no matter how many times I am trying to utter the same series of sounds, the air will always vibrate in a different way. And even if I can vibrate the air several times in roughly the same way by using a sound recording device, the nervous activity as a result of the air vibration in my brain – though it will take place about the same area of my brain – will probably not activate exactly the same nerve cells. If I am observing the feeling generated in me from my own point of view, I will still notice small differences when I hear the same word several times one after the other. If I were to examine the process of how I depict the phenomena of the world and what series of sounds I assign to them from the point of view of an theoretician, my hair would stand on end (if I had any, that is).

I see something that I only roughly see, and what I eventually see only exists in me and the only person that sees this something as I do is me. Now I assign a series of feelings of sound to what I have seen but this series of feelings of sound only exists in me and everyone else feels it in a different way, and what they feel in a different way is different indeed each and every time they feel it. Now, analyse that!

How can you learn about the world, how can you create words and how can you make logical operations with those words? One of the reasons for the inaccuracy of thinking with words is the inaccuracy of the words themselves. A reason why sciences have seen such a dramatic development is that they use much more accurate words than social studies. But the problem of the accuracy of words is only one of the factors that influence the effectiveness of our thinking. I am suggesting, however, that we should carry on our research in the field of accuracy. What shall we do? It is simple. We need to improve the accuracy of words.

It is clear from our new definition of a word, that you can do it in two different ways. Putting it simply but inaccurately, one of the ways to make our words more accurate is to clarify more precisely what we want to name. Putting it in a more complicated way, from the point of view of an external observer, the individual's efforts should focus on defining and isolating as accurately as possible the part of the external world with which her interactions will trigger the patterns of nervous activity to which she assigns the pattern of nervous activity induced in her by the air vibrated by another individual. From an internal point of view, I should focus my effort on defining and isolating as accurately as possible the feelings to which I assign the series of feelings of sound generated in me by another human being.

Putting simply but inaccurately, the other way of making our words more accurate is to make the pronunciation of the words more accurate. Putting it in a more complicated way, from the point of view of an external observer, the effort of the individual should be focused on vibrating the air – based on the patterns of nervous excitement triggered by the vibration of the air by people that are assigned to patterns of nervous excitement originating in interactions with the external world and to other patterns of nervous excitement – in such a way that the pattern of nervous excitement triggered in him by the air vibrated by him should be as close as possible to the pattern of nervous excitement triggered by the other person serving as the basis for the vibration of the air. From an internal point of view, I should try to reproduce the specific series of feelings of sound triggered in me by another person and assigned to feelings of sight, hearing, smelling, taste, touch, sense of temperature and other feelings so that this series of feelings of sound should show the closest possible resemblance to the original series of feelings of sound.

I need now to apologise to the dear reader but I must change style. Reading the definitions above, the dear reader must have felt that accurate phrasing makes my book rather difficult to read and understand. For the sake of a better reading experience, I will have to simplify, i.e. to put things more simply but more inaccurately.

4.

CREATING WORDS

The most important thing you need to understand is that in creating words we do nothing more than cut the world into units that are seemingly independent of one another. This cutting up is the most important part of creating words! This is where you can commit the biggest mistakes. Inaccurate, insufficiently defined pieces cause the greatest blunders of thinking with words.

"Oh, come on! Why are you whining about it so much? This one is a pair of sausages and that one is a mug of beer." someone might say. However, it is not that simple. Cutting the world into pieces can sometimes become rather complicated, arbitrary and inaccurate in terms of both space and time. Let us take the example of an apple. When do you start calling an apple an apple and when do you stop calling it an apple? Is it already an apple when the stamen fertilises the stigma? Or only when it has a proper apple shape? Or only when it is no longer green? Or only when it is separated from the apple tree? After the apple is separated from the apple tree, how long will it still be an apple? Since from the moment of separation, the slow but certain dissolution of the apple starts.

And in terms of space, why and where is an apple an apple? When an apple is still on the apple tree, is it only a part of the apple tree? Does it mean that we cannot talk about a separate apple at all, only a red, round part of the apple tree? And the sunbeams that enter the apple to a depth of a couple of millimetres, are they part of the apple or part of the sun?

As a matter of fact, the growth of the apple is a natural process that takes place in time, and the soil, the air and the rays of our sun all participate in this process. We people do not do anything but cut these uniform and indivisible processes that take place in time and space arbitrarily into inaccurately defined units to which we assign series of feelings of sound. Creating words in the perfect way is a hopeless enterprise in the first place as we try to divide the indivisible. That is, we try to do the impossible and look puzzled when it does not work. It is like trying to square the circle. We need words, however, because we cannot cope without them. There is therefore nothing left to do but to try and be as accurate as possible whilst being aware of the mistakes you are inevitably going to commit.

Undoubtedly, it is our sight that plays the biggest role in cutting the world around us into pieces. Cutting the world into pieces based on what we see is primarily grounded in the fact that the mass of the material in the world around us is unevenly distributed. There are centres of mass formed in the space around us the mass and density, i.e. the mass per unit of volume, of which is varied. These centres of mass were the main organisers of human word creation, especially in the beginning. Let us take a tree standing at the foot of a rock as an example. The two centres of mass are neatly separated in space, in mass and in density alike. That is why it is easy to describe them with different words.

Let us examine the rock now. It is a 100-metre high, beautiful, monolithic block. We take a pneumatic hammer and chop a piece of the rock off. We call the piece we chopped a stone. We did not call the piece a stone until we chopped it off the rock, although it had been there in the huge rock all along. In order to be able to call it a stone, we first had to separate it from the rock, i.e. we had to create another centre of mass. Just like the two guys talking in the joke: "What a great piece of art the Michelangelo's *Pietà* is!" "Oh, come on! That's bullshit. The sculpture had always been there in the stone, he only had to remove the excess."

But for us people, the less dense mass filling the space between centres of mass sometimes remains invisible and unnoticed. We do not see, for example, the air between two apples, but we see the water between a fish and ourselves. Therefore, it is very probable that people created the word for water much earlier than the word for air.

Naturally, cutting the world according to centres of mass requires further qualification and fine-tuning. People started to examine what interactions various centres of mass have with them or with other centres of mass. That is, we started to examine how we see those centres of mass and what feelings they generate in us. For example, if you take a yellow piece of river gravel and a yellow apple in your hand, you will be able to differentiate between them based on what you see and what feelings are triggered in you. So you will call them different names and you will know exactly which one to eat.

Although material fills our world everywhere, the distribution of mass and density of that material, as I mentioned, is rather uneven. Our experience is that larger energies are found in and around places where the density of mass is higher than in and around places of lower density of mass. That is, larger energies are present between the molecules and atoms in the middle of a piece of stone than, for example, on the surface where the stone contacts the air, not to mention the energies between the molecules of the air. This statement seems to be true also on a larger scale. Think, for example, of planets, solar systems and black holes.

It makes sense to cut the world along already existing, natural, faultlines, i.e. to use one word to name centres of masses within which roughly the same amounts and types of energies are found or which have roughly the same amounts and types of interactions with the environment. Using the example of the stone, it would not be wise to call both the stone and the layer of air around it a stone.

Just as I mentioned above, the most important momentum in creating words is the accuracy of cutting the world. Major faultlines are usually easy to notice and discover and they have proved to be sufficient in our everyday life. We are now, however, interested in high accuracy word creation. As a matter of fact, we are examining the main principles and pitfalls of accurately cutting the world into pieces along faultlines with a doctor's scalpel.

As I said before, in order to cut the world into pieces appropriately, it is unavoidable that we thoroughly examine the interactions existing in the world. We can only do that if:

1. We interact with the part of our world we want to examine.
   In this case, we can make conclusions about the interactions between the given part of the world and ourselves on the basis of the impact the part we are examining has on us. For example, we look at something in order to find out if it emits an electromagnetic radiation or not, or if we smell, taste or touch something. What can cause inaccuracy in such an examination?
   – The biggest problem is caused by the fact that our nervous system has its limitations in terms of interacting with the world around us. Only the visible light range of the electromagnetic radiation comes into contact with our nervous system; it is only materials soluble in saliva

that we can taste; and we cannot smell certain gases and vapours. The range of interactions is limited.
- The next problem is sensitivity. Our nervous system is not activated below a certain threshold and we do not notice insignificant amounts of smells, tastes etc.
- The third problem is resolution. Our eyes, for example, can only create an image of limited resolution, i.e. we cannot differentiate between points standing too close to one another with our eyes.
- The fourth factor is dynamics. Very big and very small changes taking place in a short time remain unnoticed by us.
- The fifth factor is the time factor. We cannot notice fast changes taking place in a very short time just as we cannot notice very slow ones, either.

2. We interact with parts of our world that have been involved in interactions with the parts we want to examine. This is what happens normally, when we look at an object. As most of these objects do not emit electromagnetic radiation in the range that is visible for us, usually we only see reflected light, i.e. light the object we are examining has already had an interaction with and which has transformed it. The situation is the same with hearing. If an object is vibrating, we usually do not make direct contact with it. We only make contact with the air vibrated by the object.

In this kind of examination, however, we need to take into consideration the errors that follow from the laws of physics, for example that light bends under the impact of a strong field of gravity, or the speed and direction of our movement has an influence on the pitch of sound, etc.

Mapping the interactions is made even harder because errors add up. The first distortion of data may take place when the transmission medium comes into contact with the phenomenon we are examining and until we notice this change. The second distortion may occur when we make direct contact with the transmission medium. For example we hear the sound of the whistle of a train that is moving away from us at a lower pitch due to the speed of the train, or softer due to the fog and, in any case, we can only hear a part of it because of the limited bandwidth of our ears.

After trying to minimise the errors made during examination, the next step is to try and establish an order among the interactions found in the part of the world we are examining. From the given interactions, we select the ones that are the most typical of the given phenomenon, then the ones that are less typical of them and finally the ones that are the least typical. For example, when we are examining a piece of iron, we find that the most typical interaction of that particular piece of iron is the connection between the iron atoms and not the connection between the iron atoms and other contaminating particles. We may also find that, although there are a few oxygen atoms within the block of iron, it is not at all a typical feature of it. Most of the oxygen atoms are to be found on the surface of the block of iron in the form of iron oxide, i.e. common rust. There are more oxygen atoms on the surface of the iron block but not all of them are connected to an iron atom. Some of the oxygen atoms are connected to other oxygen atoms and they sometimes leave the surface. Not only oxygen atoms but also hydrogen, nitrogen and rare gas atoms are moving around the surface. And we haven't even mentioned the electromagnetic radiations and particle radiations, nor the field of gravity within the piece of iron.

And the time will come when you need to make a decision and you need to take the scalpel and cut: when you need to decide that you call things in one direction from a certain point of the world by one name and things in the other direction by another name. And the stronger the magnifying glass you are using, the harder the job is!

The train of thoughts described above can also easily be

used in the field of sciences. When we denote different particles, molecules, cells, internal organs or living creatures with different words, we can cope relatively easily, exactly because these parts of our world are relatively simple to separate from their environment. But what is the case with human studies? The situation is much more complicated here. This method is completely impossible to use in the field of human studies. Or is it? In the field of human studies, it is completely impossible to define what faith, plea, morals, sin or punishment are. Or is it? Interesting questions, are they not? But let us not rush. Let us go step by step.

The next step in creating words is to assign a series of feelings of sound to the given part of the world we have cut into pieces. This process took a different form in each part of our planet. That is how different languages were formed. But it is not only linguistic differences that we can observe but, if we go back a little to the previous topic, we can also find differences coming from cutting the world into pieces in different ways. For example, the average Central European has only one word for rice, whereas people living in the Far East use many more. The same applies to the Eskimos who use a range of words for snow. A well-educated, modern European who speaks English cuts the world into pieces in an entirely different way than an uneducated person from the jungle from the Middle Ages (I used English as an example because it has a wide range of vocabulary).

It is also important to point out that even people coming from the same cultural background with a similar level of education do not cut the world into pieces in exactly the same way. Although they use roughly the same series of feelings of sound to denote certain pieces of the world, the cutting itself they do not do along exactly the same lines. So the meaning of the words is a little bit different for each of them. But the important thing is not only that the people using the same language should cut the world into pieces in a similar way, but also that they can reproduce the series of feelings of sound assigned to each part with a relatively high accuracy. Errors of reproduction typical of a certain region will result in regional dialects, some of which may be so disturbing that they make it difficult to identify and understand some of the words.

So the individuals also commit errors during the reproduction of series of feelings of sound – not only when cutting the world into pieces – and these errors then accumulate. As a matter of fact, the ideal solution would be if the whole of humankind used the same language without any dialects in the same cultural background at the same level of education. This is still a bit further away, I am afraid.

5.

LEVELS OF EXAMINING EVENTS

People 'play' the jigsaw puzzle called 'Learning about the world' on multiple levels. These levels build on one another and are organically interrelated: grow in one another and overlap. Let us see what these levels are:

Philosophy
Sociology
Psychology
Something
Biology
Chemistry
Physics

Do not worry! I know the list is far from being complete. But I suggest that we move on and see what comes out of it at the end. Let us start with the basics at the bottom of the list.

Why is physics the basis of everything? Because this is the science that examines what subatomic particles atoms are built up from. The interactions between subatomic particles define the structure of the atoms. Why is it important to know the structure of the atoms accurately? Because this is what defines how the atoms are connected to one another.

Why is it important to know how the atoms are connected? Because atoms connected in different ways build up different elements and compounds that have completely different characteristics than the individual atoms they are made of. The interactions between the atoms of the different elements will define what new compounds are formed. And these compounds are what the science of chemistry is concerned with.

Why is it important to be aware of the structure and characteristics of compounds? Because living creatures consist of complex compounds. The interaction between the various compounds is the basis of life. Biochemistry is the science that examines what interactions these various complex compounds have with one another and how they are connected to one another in living creatures.

Why is it important to know how the complex compounds are connected to one another in living creatures? Because these compounds build up the organs of living creatures, and the operations and interactions of the system of these organs is what biology is concerned with. Apart from the chemical control, it is the nervous system that is responsible for the control of human organs, and the examination of the nervous system is the field of research of a special sub-branch of biology called neurology.

Why is it important to have detailed knowledge about the human nervous system? Because it is during the interactions between the various nerve cells that the '**somethings**' are formed. And now, my dear readers, we have arrived at '**something**'. To what? It is easy to guess. To **something** of which the operation of the nervous system forms the basis. To **something** the existence of which science has disregarded for centuries like devil shuns incense. The **something** that has been there in front of our eyes since humans became human but we did not notice it, or if we noticed it, we did not pay attention.

Well, this **something** is the basis of the acts and behaviour of each and every person and it is psychology that is responsible for analysing it. It is, of course, a different question how successful they are, if they do not even know the rudiments. It is the science of psychology that should study human behaviour on the basis of the interactions of these **somethings**. Psychology serves, or rather should serve, as the basis of social studies in general: sociology that is responsible for studying social behaviour on the basis of interactions between human beings; cultural anthropology; history; art history; political studies; legal studies; economic studies; linguistics and, what is considered the science of all sciences, philosophy.

All this somehow reminds me of an old trip of mine. A long time ago I visited one of my friends in Washington who happened to be living in a building of 20 or 21 floors. Why 20 or 21? Because there was no 13th floor in the building. Or there was, but still there was not. There was no button for floor 13 in the elevator. Button 14 was right next to button 12. At first, I thought something was wrong with my eyes, so I got out at the 14th floor and walked down the steps and, surprise-surprise, I immediately found myself on the 12th floor. As it turned out later on, they did not use number 13 out of superstition.

As you very well know, it is actually impossible to construct a building that has 12 floors with 3 metres of air above it where the wind blows through and with the 14th floor and the rest of the building just hanging over it. This is nonsense. However, humankind is trying to do this kind of trick. Let me share a secret with you: it will not work. Many may not like it, many may think I am mean or even something more serious but, like it or not, that is the case.

Of course you do not need to accept it. You can have your doubts. You can ignore it. You can hate it or scold it. Just take your turn. And time is passing slowly, tick-tock, tick-tock. And millions of people die of starvation, of poverty and in wars. Tick-tock, tick-tock. And the time will come (at least, I hope it will) when people will exclaim: "Look, we have not noticed the 13th floor!"

Why will the process of recognition be so hard? Because, with the appearance of our '**something**', we will have to re-think each and every bit of art, politics, social studies and, in general, the whole of human life. And many people will not like it. There is, of course, no reason to hurry. We have enough time. Tick-tock, tick-tock. But for now, I suggest that we move on.

Let us examine the different levels of science in a little more detail. What are the characteristics of each one of them? One of the most important things that strikes the eye is that each one of them has its special vocabulary typical of that particular level alone. But it is not only the vocabulary, but also the system of logical connections that is different. People 'living' or working in a given level do not do anything else but 'play chess' with the vocabulary of the given level. That is, they carry out logical operations with the words according to the rules of the given level.

One single person cannot know the vocabulary and the logical connections between the words of every level. Apart from the vocabulary and logical connections of everyday life, today's average person knows the vocabulary of a special subfield of only one or two levels. Now, you cannot make operations with words that you do not know. You cannot use them because they do not exist for you. In your thinking, you can only use words that you know and only when you also know how they connect to one another. Let us look at an example. I do not want to offend any of my readers but I suppose most of you have not heard about quarks or gluons. These words are only empty series of sounds for you that you are reading for the first time. And since this is the first time you have met them, you could not have made logical operations with them. And not only could you not think with them, but you could not think about them either as these words simply did not exist for you. Now you can think about them but you still cannot think with them. What does it mean to think about them? It means, for example, to think something like "Listen, how nice they sound! 'Quark' reminds me of the sound of a frog." You will only be able to think with them if we fill these empty series of feelings of sound with meaning, i.e. if we assign these series of feelings of sounds to some pieces of the world and say, for example, that these are particles. This time, we can think with them on the level of everyday life: "Oh, so these are the small thingies that must be flying around". This, however, is not enough for success. Not enough, because without knowing the characteristics of these particles, we cannot work with them, we cannot make logical operations with them. In order to do so, we need to know that these particles are the building blocks of protons and neutrons, we need to know their specific mass, that they do not have an electrical charge, how long their life cycle is, etc. Only then can we work with them. We can define and calculate how they would behave in certain situations.

Events can be examined at the level of multiple sciences at the same time. The first level is the one you can describe with the science of physics. At this level, we examine processes and interactions in which new elements are created but new compounds are not. So, for example, we create the atoms of an element by bombing an atom of another element, or we can examine gravity, different kinds of radiations, particles and so on. When a proton hits a nucleus, this event takes place in the field of physics. The field of chemistry cannot do anything with this event, not to mention biology. For the sciences of chemistry and biology, this interaction or event is impossible to interpret.

At the second level, we examine interactions and events during which new compounds are created. This is the level the science of chemistry is concerned with. If a new compound is created in the test tube of a chemist, this event takes place in the field, or or at the level, of chemistry. You need to see, however, that biology cannot do anything with this event either. At the level of biology this event is impossible to interpret but it is at possible to interpret it at the level of physics. The level of physics can give an explanation of why the atoms of the compound are connected to each other exactly the way are. As a matter of fact, two sciences examine this level. They are physics and chemistry, since it is physics that is concerned with the atoms the new compounds are created from. A conscientious chemist has no chance of completely understanding the world of compounds if she does not know on what principles the atoms of various elements are connected.

The third level is examined by biology, which deals with living creatures. A psychologist cannot interpret the operation of one nerve cell because the interactions and processes taking place within a nerve cell are carried out at the biology level. But a physician and a chemist could have some relevant ideas. So, this field is actually examined by three different sciences.

As we move up through the levels of sciences, more and more fields of science are involved in the examination of a given interaction, event or phenomenon. It is because the smallest building elements of the material world are subatomic particles which then, building on top of one another, create more and more complicated units, and the fields of sciences, following this practice, also build organically on one another or grow out of one another. Taking a building as an analogy, it is just like the way different floors are built on top of one another. And the 3rd floor of a building can only exist if it is supported by 2nd floor which is, in turn, supported by the 1st floor. 3rd floor – or 13rd floor, for that matter – does not just usually hang in mid-air.

It is a different issue that humankind, during its history, was forced to try and build the fortress of science at each level at the same time and not from bottom to top as a builder would do it. So it was not as though a prehistoric man went to his favourite cyclotron, switched it on and, on a gloomy autumn day, discovered the deepest secrets of the structure of matter and the next day cooked up a synthetic DNA chain while sitting among his favourite test tubes and then, on the third day, created the first artificial cell. The learning process took place at the same time at each level of the sciences involving many trials and errors. And since the entire process went on without sound foundations and without the levels organically built on those foundations, sometimes entire levels collapsed, and they had to restart everything from square one. It is exactly like when a builder does not start building at the foundation but begins to build all the levels at the same time. This usually does not work. But it is natural. There was no extraterrestrial civilisation to show us the right way.

As humankind's knowledge grew, the faster and more strongly the different levels of sciences were connected to one another. You may ask now why we need chemistry and biology at all, if we can describe all these interactions and processes at the level of physics. Because it would be unproductive, cumbersome and complicated. It would be the same Sisyphean job as building a 20 (or 21) storey building atom by atom. We use blocks instead. We bake bricks from the molecules of clay, build flats from the bricks and build the building from the flats one on top of another. One of the builders is only concerned with how to make bricks from the clay. She does not care at all what others will do with the bricks and how they will use them. This builder lives in 'the world of bricks' and she is only interested in what processes take place within the brick. Another builder lives in 'the world of the flat'. He is only interested in what happens within a flat: what rooms there are and how they are laid out in comparison with another. The third builder thinks on the level of the building. She does not care what happens within a flat, not to mention the processes taking place within the brick. And here we have arrived at an important moment. The consequence of thinking in blocks is that with your blocks, you can only describe or explain phenomena above the level using the given blocks. In other words, with the blocks used on the level of the building, I can describe the internal composition of a town but not the internal structure of a building. If I am interested in the internal structure of the building, I need to go down at least one level. With the blocks used on the level of the flats, I can already describe the building and the conditions within the building. That is, in a perfectly understandable way, you cannot build the smaller blocks from the bigger blocks, only the other way round. But you cannot make a certain sized block from other blocks of the same size, either. The only thing you can do is replace one with the other.

In turn, the consequence of the above statements is that you cannot explain words on the level of words. No matter how nicely you twist your words, how breathtakingly logical are the constructions you create, how round the definitions you come up with, you will not get closer to truth. The world of thinking in words that is, naturally, based on words, cannot be understood without examining what words themselves consist of, i.e. what building blocks you use to build words. However, this is what humankind is trying to do. And we are also trying to skip the science of '**something**', or the 13th floor, and are trying to find explanations directly on the level of neurobiology.

If we want to find our way in the world of thinking in words, we need to start our examination a little further down, i.e. on the 13th floor, on the level of the science of '**something**'. Of course, we are going to use words on the 13th floor as well but these are going to be words that describe the blocks and relations of that floor: the series of feelings of sounds assignable to the blocks to be found on the 13th floor. But let us now move on.

People used the same cutting and breaking of the world into pieces seen in word creation also when forming the fields of science. Because what is science? Science is nothing other than cutting the uniform world into pieces and examining the interactions of the broken pieces. Since the broken pieces must be denoted in some way, possibly with words, and also the interactions between them should be denoted in some way, something we do with words again, science can be considered the greatest word creation activity.

Science, however did not only cut the world into pieces but also cut the process of learning into comfortable pieces, easily overviewed by one person. Naturally, the more we know about the world, the smaller the pieces we break it up into and the smaller the pieces we break sciences into as well. Scientists are only slightly interested in what is going on in another block. Each one of them concentrates primarily on his or her own block, and builds things from materials available there. Each scientific level has its own vocabulary. If you check the vocabulary of the scientific levels, you will see that the words they apply have different levels of tolerance and accuracy. The difference in accuracy is the most striking if we have a look at the two fields that are the farthest apart: physics and philosophy. Let us take, for example the world 'hydrogen' from physics and the word 'spirit' from philosophy. The content of the word 'hydrogen' is defined with a much higher accuracy than that of the word 'spirit'. If somebody asks what we should assign the sound series 'hydrogen' to, we ask a physician to explain the structure of the hydrogen atom and the characteristics of its components inside out. But what will a philosopher answer if we ask her what does she assign the sound series 'spirit' to? Well, the answer will be some inconceivable explanation that would fill pages, or in a worse case, even books. If we examine the accuracy of the words of the different levels, we will see that the accuracy of the words will decrease at an approximately even pace moving from physics to biology. The meanings of the words become increasingly blurred, i.e. their accuracy decreases, whereas their tolerance increases. Let us take as an example the word 'hydrogen' from physics, the word 'plastic' from chemistry and the word 'heart' from biology. This process is understandable, since when we break our world into pieces, the bigger the piece we are breaking, the more ways there are to do the breaking and the more sub-parts each part may have. When we increase the number of components, the errors add up and the inaccuracy of the final outcome increases and the accuracy of our words decreases.

Although the accuracy of breaking the world into pieces decreases as we move away from the base, i.e. from bottom to top, it also increases as time passes and as sciences evolve. It is proven by the great achievements sciences have produced.

It is perfectly obvious, but still often escapes our attention, that the borders between levels of sciences are only penetrable in one direction: from bottom to top. In other words, I cannot describe the processes taking place in an atom with the words polymer and heart, however, I can describe the processes taking place in a polymer or a heart with the words used at the atomic or subatomic level. It is a different issue that it is a very difficult, almost Sisyphean task. This is exactly the error generations of philosophers have committed throughout the centuries of our history. Not only did they use inaccurate words, but they also tried to do the impossible, i.e. to explain the world from top to bottom. They were trying to build the smaller parts of the jigsaw puzzle from the bigger ones. As if they were building a flat from a building, a brick from a flat or a molecule from a brick. Well, this does not usually work. Do not misunderstand me, we must not judge them for it! They did their job. They were making an effort. They were not just being idle, rather they were trying to learn about the world with all the means they had, and this deserves praise, and suits us humans. You must never judge someone for thinking, for using his or her brain. It is a much bigger problem if someone does not do so.

Let us now get back to level 13 or, to be more accurate to the level of '**something**'. The level of 'something' is a level of extraordinary importance. This is what decides the fate of humankind. "COM'ON! Don't come with this shit!" Many of my readers must now be thinking. All I can answer to this is "YES, INDEED!" Let us see what grounds I have for my statement.

The attentive reader must have noticed that in the previous parts I only dealt with the first three sciences: physics, chemistry and biology. What is the reason? The reason is that the inaccuracy of the words dramatically increases in sciences above the level of biology. And the consequence of this fact is that the way people think also becomes extraordinarily inaccurate and chaotic in the levels above biology. This theory is supported by the fact that whereas there are only a couple of, or sometimes only one, theories to describe a phenomenon in the fields of physics, chemistry or biology, there are dozens, or sometimes hundreds, of theories to describe a phenomenon in the levels above biology.

My dear reader may now rightly think that it is natural since, as we leave biology, we come across an increasing number of complex phenomena put together from various components and that is why it is reasonable that multiple theories are born. It is truly so, however, that the accuracy of words above the level of biology does not decrease evenly but exponentially and drastically. There must be a reason behind this sudden and abrupt change. The answer lies at the 13th floor.

6.

THE 13TH FLOOR

I hope everyone is now really curious to see what on earth is on the 13ᵗʰ floor. Well, my dear readers, let us pay a visit there. If we get in the elevator, there, just above the button for the 12ᵗʰ floor, there is a tiny button (not everyone notices it) with a hardly visible number 13 on it. This is what you need to push. When the door of the elevator opens, our eyes look on the floor and we notice that it is covered with a thick layer of dust. We discover a few tentative footprints in the dust starting from the elevator door but turning back after shorter or longer distances. Somebody has been here before us! There are both very old and new footsteps among them but each of them turns back. There is not one track that leads to the rooms in the distant darkness. When we raise our eyes, we see the sign: the level of **FEELINGS**.

So, we have arrived. This is the forgotten, sometimes consciously ignored and hushed level that was even despised, scorned and forbidden in some periods of our history. The oldest footprints are the ones of the Greek philosophers, but they turned back soon. But not only did they turn back, they also declared this level filthy, chaotic, inferior, amoral and a place to avoid in their writings. They championed the theory that reason should control and master feelings. Christianity only further degraded the reputation of the world of feelings. Concepts like evil desire, evil feelings and evil pleasures appeared. These religion-related judgements did not only appear but were also implanted into generations of people for centuries. These concepts have become intertwined with our everyday life, thoughts and behaviour. And – let us admit it – for many, it is not only the past but also the present. Then, we find the footprints of Descartes, Freud, Kant, Nietzsche, Spinoza, Wittgenstein and others. With all due respect, I still need to say that the 13th floor has not yet been discovered. In order to understand the situation, we must go back to the basics.

If I wanted to be concise and easy to understand, I would say we people are controlled by both our hearts and our minds. It often happens that we do not know whether we should listen to our hearts or our minds (my lady readers must be taking a deep breath and nodding approvingly). And this is indeed the case. There is a feeling-based and a symbol-based controller within us. The feeling-based controller was formed at an earlier stage of our evolution than the symbol-based controller. A similar process takes place during our individual development. The behaviour of the baby, until she learns to speak, is driven by her feelings. The same was the case with prehistoric people. They were also controlled by their feelings and symbol-based control was only gradually developed with the appearance of words, i.e. symbols, and the development of the human language. So we might declare the feeling-based control was the primary one of the two.

But how does it work in everyday life? How do these two controllers guide us? In close cooperation. The most trivial case is when we have a feeling of hunger and ask the question: "Darling, what kind of food do we have at home?" And when we see the empty refrigerator, we decide that we should go down to the grocery store. We tend to use the symbol-based control primarily to satisfy our needs, in close cooperation with the feeling-based control. It is also through our feeling-based control that we learn about the existence and the current status of our needs (see the example above).

However, the intensity and the closeness of this cooperation varies. When we are driving a car, where the feeling-based controller dominates, we can easily think about complex problems with the help of our symbol-based controller. And we can do this for kilometres at a time so that we do not even remember what we saw on our way. In such a case, the two systems operate independently from one another. However, if something unusual happens while driving, something that requires the intervention of the symbol-based controller – diverted traffic or a particularly pretty lady etc. – then the symbol-based controller puts the current train of thoughts aside and solves the problem in cooperation with the feeling-based controller. Once the problem is solved, the control centres loosen their connection and we can go back to the original status. That is what happens to us day by day: while we are thinking about the daily toil of life or considering elaborate economic, artistic, religious or philosophic reasoning, we do not pay attention to our feelings. And our feelings do their job very neatly: they drive the 'car' and control our life.

Our feelings are always with us, only we do not always focus our attention on our feelings. To make it easier to understand, I could compare feelings to air. Many of us do not think of the word 'air' for days, weeks or even months. For us, air does not exist, so to speak. It does not exist because we do not see it, do not hear it, do not touch it and do not smell it. Or, to be more precise, we do touch it, but when we touch it we do not say "the air is flowing", we say "the wind is blowing" instead. When we smell the air, we say "something is stinking", instead of saying "other molecules are mixed with the molecules of air". When we feel hot or cold, we say "it is hot or cold" and not that "the kinetic energy of the molecules of air has increased or decreased". But who would dare to doubt the existence of air? Without air, we could not live. We inhale air, we take oxygen from air even through our skin, its molecules support our skin, otherwise we would blow up in the vacuum, we swim in the air and we live in and by it. Just as air does not exist for us, so to speak; similarly, the feelings we experience when breathing do not exist for us either. If you now take a deep breath attentively, you will experience how air flows into your body through your nose and how it fills your lungs through your throat while your chest is expanding. These feelings, however, all remain unnoticed in our everyday life, which, of course, does not mean that they do not exist. They do exist, just as air does.

Or, for example, you must be feeling now that the chair you are sitting in is pushing your bum. You are feeling it because the attention of your symbol-based controller is focused on your bum. But you should not forget that you felt the same 10 minutes ago, only you did not pay attention. The feeling existed in the same way. What is more, it did not escape the attention of your feeling-based controller if you were sitting uncomfortably, because you changed your sitting position without even noticing it at the level of your symbol-based controller. You are now reading this book, but there are many other things at the edges of your field of vision that you do not pay attention to, or do not even notice, although you see them. And most probably, you are not sitting in a silent room so you are hearing the noises of your environment, but you do not notice them because you are not paying attention. When you are eating and you do something important at the same time, you do not even notice the taste of food. But this, naturally, does not mean that there is no sense of taste present.

So far, we have only been dealing with feelings that are generated in us in connection with the external world but we have not talked about the other parts of feelings that give information to us about our internal world or that guide and control us. For 99% of people, these feelings simply do not exist. Or rather, they do exist indeed, but we – as in the examples above – simply do not take notice of them. Only the most intensive feelings such as hunger, thirst, pain, tiredness, sleepiness or the need to defecate are exceptions. But even in these trivial cases, we are not conscious that these are feelings. We say we are hungry, we are thirsty instead of saying we are experiencing the feeling of hunger or the feeling of thirst.

For people who live 99.9% of their life at the level of the symbol-based controller, it is like a lost world, as if it did not exist at all. But it does exist, it is there in each and every one of us, only you need to pay attention. We do not deal with things the existence of which we do not know about, and we cannot know things we do not deal with. This was partly the reason why humankind did not explore the connections within the complex system of feelings. The other part of the reason was – as I mentioned previously – that the world of feelings was implanted into people's minds as a detestable, inferior, filthy and evil territory that must be avoided.

My book *Feelings* (Copyright © Margóczi Győző 2016, ISBN 978-963-12-4878-4) makes an attempt to classify and systematise feelings on the basis of their functions. *Feelings* explores in depth how feelings function and how they control our life. I wanted to make this reference because, although I am trying to write in a simple language, as we move on I will have to use some new terminology and new words the explanation and detailed description of which you will find in my book *Feelings*. This strategy is necessary because of the limited size of this book. But let us move on.

Now, I would like to call your attention to a special field of feelings, namely the feelings of sound, or to put it more simply: sounds. Some of you must be asking now why sounds would be feelings. I am suggesting that you try to recall memories from the past and do a couple of simple experiments. The simplest and most graphic example for the feeling of sound is a rock concert. Standing in front of the huge PA speakers, you must have felt that the bass was pounding in your chest and your entire body was shaking when the drummer hit a little harder. Yes, I know that this is an extreme example but since it is extreme, it is really graphic. As a matter of fact, in rock concerts, the vibration of the air not only stimulates our auditory nerves but also stimulates other nerve endings in our body through which we feel the vibrations.

A less extreme example, and another experiment, to examine the feelings of sound is a sound generator. I know it is not typical that every family has a sound generator somewhere among the jam jars in the larder but you can easily download a sound generator program from the Internet to your computer. Now put on your headphones and start listening to sounds at different pitches and at different volumes. Let each pitch sound for at least 10 seconds or even longer at the same volume. You will feel it and you will understand. But in order to help you, let me give you some advice on how to analyse the findings of the experiment. There are many, many feelings present in us at any one instant. We need to select the subject of our examination from them. Sometimes we can do it, sometimes we cannot. When examining the feelings of hearing, the easiest feeling to notice is the feeling of sound itself, i.e. the feeling of the sound growling or ringing in our ear. This is the feeling we should concentrate on in our experiment.

However, another feeling also appears, with more or less intensity, that 'tells us' if we find the given feeling of sound nice and beautiful or unpleasant. I called these types of feelings 'orienting feelings' because they orientate and guide our attention to things that are useful and keep us away from things that are useless or even harmful for us. For many, it is difficult to separate and differentiate these two types of feelings without sufficient practice. And I also need to mention the feeling of pain. If you set the level of volume too high, you can experience pain in your ear. The feeling of pain is nothing else but the 'need indicating feeling' of security. If your ear is already ringing from all the growling or screaming sounds, you can take off your headphones.

During the experiment we might also have experienced that after a given sound started, a little time had to pass before we could focus our attention on the sound. In other words, we had been listening to the sound 'for quite a time' by the time we could focus our attention on the feeling itself. If the sound is not long enough, we simply do not have the time to focus our attention on it because the sound is not there anymore. That does not mean, however, that the feeling of sound had never been present. It only means that the process of focusing our attention took longer than the presence of the feeling of sound. A consequence of the above is that if we hear a non-rhythmic series of many different short sounds, we cannot follow the series of feelings with our attention because the inertia of our attention is bigger than our ability to separate the different feelings of sounds. But that does not mean that the sounds following one another are not feelings. You cannot disprove the presence of feelings of sound anyway, because – as we explained in the beginning of this book – sounds do not exist outside us, human beings. On the other side of our eardrum, there are only vibrations of the air. If you do not have feelings of sound, it only means that the ocean of air on the other side of your eardrum is still.

From the previous paragraphs, we can draw the conclusion that **words are nothing else but series of feelings**. The words we use in speech we do not consider feelings because the shortness of the sounds following one another in each of the words does not allow us to focus our attention on the short pieces of feelings. But that does not mean that words are not series of feelings. And the consequence of the previous statement is that our **thoughts are chains of series of feelings of sound**. So the scientists who are examining the activity of different parts of the human brain with their equipment during thinking and speaking must be looking for feelings and specifically: series of feelings of sound. For those who still doubt that words are nothing else but series of feelings of sound, I would suggest a simple experiment. Ask a friend to pronounce a word sound by sounds so that each sound lasts at least 10 seconds. Let us take the word 'apple' as an example: aaaaaaaaaaaaaaaaaaa-ppppppppppppppppppp-lllllllllllllllllllllllllllll. Of course, it may be useful to explain the point of the experiment to your friend, lest he had doubts about your state of mind. Naturally, you can also use some sound recording device and listen to your own voice. We need an external sound source because the vibrations generated in our own throat are passed on to the neighbouring tissue and, through the skull bone, they eventually reach our ears and that might disturb our experiment.

For an external observer, the definition of a word at the levels of the different sciences is as follows: at the level of the science of feelings, a word is nothing else but "A series of feelings of sound – triggered in a person by a specific vibration of the air created by another person – that is assigned to feelings created in the person as a result of the electromagnetic radiation, the chemical compounds and the pressure of the external world, the vibration of the gas molecules that constitute the air and the impact that changes the kinetic energy of the surface of the skin or as a result of internal changes."

At the higher level of neurobiology, the definition of a word would be similar to the one that we gave at the beginning of our book: "A pattern of nervous excitement – triggered in a person by a specific vibration of the air created by another person – that is assigned to another pattern of nervous excitement created in the person as a result of the electromagnetic radiation, the chemical compounds and the pressure of the external world, the vibration of the gas molecules that constitute the air and the impact that changes the kinetic energy of the surface of the skin or as a result of internal changes."

At the lower level of neurobiology, in order to give a definition, we should specifically define the nerve cells that contribute with their excitement to hearing a word, memorising it or recalling it from our memory. At even lower levels of biology, we should define the structure and composition of the cells that participate in forming a word. At the level of chemistry we should define the compounds that constitute the cells in question. At the level of physics we should define the atoms that constitute the compounds under examination. At the level of nuclear physics we should define the subatomic particles that constitute the given atoms.

It is clear from the previous paragraphs that we can define the word 'word' relatively accurately when we are moving downwards through the levels of sciences. But what is the case if we start moving upwards from the level of the science of feelings? If I wanted to be brief, I would say there is a huge mess above the level of the science of feelings. Why? Because it is at the level of feelings where we change dimensions, where the mapping of the world around us is separated from the imaginary world. Or rather, it should be separated because actually, it is mixed up with it, and this is exactly what causes the mess.

7.

CHANGE OF DIMENSIONS

If we are creating words, we should also use them. Our goal, however, is not just to use them 'somehow' but to use them to describe the world around us and come to conclusions about the events of the present and the future. Although using inappropriate words, or using words inappropriately, can play tricks on us and, in the worst case, can also have severe consequences. The source of such severe consequences may be the change of dimensions. Let us look at an extreme example.

Mary and Gabriel live in two villages 17 km apart from one another. They agreed to meet each other by phone but since Mary had a busy schedule, she could not tell when she would be able to start so she asked Gabriel to start walking towards her and they would meet somewhere on the way. Gabriel started immediately after their discussion on the phone and did 3 km an hour. As luck would have it, though, Mary could only start an hour after their discussion on the phone because she had to help her mother with the housework. Mary did 4 km an hour. The question is when and where did Mary and Gabriel meet?

It is quite clear that Mary and Gabriel had to do 17 km altogether to their meeting point because that is the distance between the two villages. Gabriel's part of the 17 km equals the distance he could do in an hour multiplied by the time that passed since the time he had started. So if you mark the time that had passed since he started with the letter t, the distance Gabriel did equals t x 3 km.

The above statements are equally applicable to Mary, although Mary started an hour later so she was moving for a shorter period than Gabriel. She was walking for exactly one hour less. So we can get the time she spent walking if we deduct an hour from the time Gabriel spent walking: t-1 hour. If we multiply the time Mary spent walking by the distance she could cover in an hour, we will get the distance Mary walked which is: (t – 1) x 4. As we know that the distance between the two villages is 17 km and we know that Mary and Gabriel eventually met each other, it is clear that the total distance the two of them did was 17 km, so (t – 1) x 4 + t x 3 = 17 km. Now let us try to solve the equation 4(t – 1) + 3t = 17.

And here comes everything! This is the point where we lost contact with reality or rather with logically following the events that took place in reality. From this point on, we act like a machine: we only carry out a routine procedure, a program that has absolutely nothing to do with the processes taking place in the real world. There is no Mary anymore and no Gabriel, just as there is no distance and no village with smoking chimneys and storks on top of them. There is nothing else but numbers and rigid algebra. In other words, we change dimensions.

Well, let's get started:

I rearrange the left-hand side of our equation:
4t – 4 + 3t = 17
I reduce the left-hand side:
7t – 4 = 17
Then I take -4 from the left-hand side of the equation to

the right-hand side but I change the sign in the meantime:

$7t = 17 + 4$

I reduce the right-hand side of our equation:

$7t = 21$

I take 7 from the left-hand side to the right-hand side but since it was a multiplier on the left-hand side, it is going to become a factor on the right-hand side:

$t = 21 / 7$

And I do the division:

$t = 3$

But let us now go back to the real world. It turned out that Gabriel walked for 3 hours and, during these 3 hours, he did 3 times 3 km, i.e. 9 km altogether, whereas Mary only walked 2 hours and she did 8 km during those 2 hours before she met Gabriel. And they lived happily ever after.

Did we solve the exercise properly? Yes, we did. Then what is the problem? The problem is that, while we were doing the exercise, we got separated from following the actual processes: we changed dimensions, so to speak. We were doing the exercise correctly in the new dimension of algebra and we got a correct result but... What happens if you make a mistake in the dimension of algebra which is separated from the real world? Let us say we miss a sign. Of course we get the wrong result. But since we are in a different dimension, we cannot continuously check our steps in real-time. That is why we will not notice the errors we make. Naturally, we can check our calculations when we get back to the real world but we do not always do it in real life, either because we cannot do it or, as you will see later on, sometimes we expressly try to avoid checking things.

We come across the change of dimension we observed in the example above in sterile laboratory conditions also in our everyday life, even if it is not that evident. Let us look at another example. A lady is telling the following story to her friend: "Just imagine this: I was walking home the other day and a black cat ran across the street right in front of me. When I got home I tried to unlock our front door but it wasn't locked! But I remembered clearly that I had locked the door. Was there a burglar in our flat? I went in softly and carefully and I heard strange noises coming from the direction of the bedroom. I sneaked in there and – you won't believe it – my husband was there lying naked in the bed with the wife of our neighbour. The word 'morals' means nothing to that bastard! He had sworn to be faithful to me 'till death us part' and there he was breaking his promise! He's guilty. And if he's guilty, he must be punished. And punished he will be, indeed. I will sue him out of his house and car and everything he has, I won't even leave a pair of pants for him! He'll be begging me for mercy but I'll be laughing in his face. Guys like him should learn properly what love is. I've called my lawyer and I'm seeing him tomorrow afternoon. I don't know what I should put on, maybe that cute little dress you saw me in last time..."

I suppose my dear reader has noticed where the change of dimension took place. Yes, the lady moved to another dimension where she operates with concepts like love, faith, swearing, morals, guilt and punishment. She establishes logical relationships between these words, she draws a conclusion, she makes a judgement and she acts accordingly (and, of course, she is preaching about love, while blood is dripping off her vampire's teeth).

Why could changing dimensions be problematic? Why might it be dangerous? Because we separate ourselves from the real world, the level where things actually take place. And this is exactly the problem with the work of the great thinkers of humanity! Each one of their major works is packed with changes of dimensions. And as a result, they became separated from the level of the real, non-imaginary world or, more precisely, from the processes taking place in the real world they analyse.

You may rightly ask what the hell the expressions 'change

of dimensions' and 'imaginary world' mean. Let us try to find out together.

8.

THE IMAGINARY WORLD

The imaginary world is rooted in the level of feelings and that is what it lives from and lives in. I guess I should explain this. A joke comes to mind in which the teacher is trying to explain the notion of minus numbers to the children: "Children, imagine that there are 10 children in a bus. If 12 children get off the bus, 2 children will still have to get on so there is nobody on the bus." This is a very good example of what kind of thoughts can be created in our inside world. Since there are no -2 children in the world around us, they only exist as words, i.e. series of feelings of sounds, in our inside world. -2 children do not run up and down in the streets. Looking at it from an external point of view, minus children are nothing else but patterns of nervous excitement in our minds. They do not exist for the external world, just the same as there is no blue sky, birdsong, nice smell of sausages or taste of a glass of good Hungarian wine. These things only exist in us, human beings, as feelings which only appear as patterns of nervous excitement for the external world.

Now, are minus children real, or not? Do minus children exist at all? "How could they exist? What nonsense!" my dear readers may exclaim. But they do exist indeed! Only, they do not exist in the world around us but in the world within us in the form of feelings, or series of feelings of sound, to be more precise.

The inside world that we experience is also part of the world: this is something that exists, only something that exists within us. But since we exist in the world, this something exists together with us, and through us, in the world as well. Minus children are just as real as the blue sky, the birdsong, the smell of the sausage and the taste of the wine which also only exist within us and which are not any more real than the series of feelings of sound describing minus children. If we deny the existence of minus children, we should also deny the existence of the blue sky, the birdsong, the smell of the sausage and the taste of the wine.

However, whereas the feelings of the blue sky, the birdsong, the smell of the sausage and the taste of the wine were generated within us as a result of an interaction with the external world, the series of feelings of sound 'minus children' cannot be directly assigned to any of the parts of the world around us. And that is because the object we could assign the series of feelings of sound 'minus children' to does not exist in the external world: it is something we invented, it only exist in our imagination. Just like the in the case of the words angels and fairies, you cannot assign the words 'minus children', freedom or democracy to any part of the external world. That is why I am suggesting calling these kinds of words 'imaginary words'. Exactly the way they use the term imaginary numbers in mathematics to denote unreal numbers, we should use the term imaginary word for words to which we cannot assign anything in the wold around us.

To make things clearer, I would cut the world into pieces in the following way: there is the first and largest part that is perfectly happy without us. Then, if our parents, for some reason, think that they need offspring, a small part of the world above separates somewhat from the rest and we spring into being. We, the tiny part of the world above, however, are not independent from the entire world but we constitute an organic but somewhat independent part of it which exists through continuous and permanent interactions in the world around us. With our death, this tiny, separated part of the world melts again into the great whole.

The second part of the world is a subjective internal world which exist in us and which is a mapping of the real world through its interactions with our body: a personal and unique form of the world. Let us call it the mapped world. That is the world of the blue sky and the birdsong. There are exactly as many subjective mapped worlds, as there are living beings, including animals, on the earth. This second part of the world ceases to exist at the moment of our death, at least according to our current knowledge.

The third part of the world is the imaginary world which also exists but which has practically nothing to do with the world around us. This is the word we ourselves create without getting our body into interaction with the world around us. Therefore, let us call this world the imaginary world. This is the world of angels and fairies or the world of words like 'minus children', freedom and democracy. This world belongs exclusively to conscious living beings and does not exist for animals. Naturally, this world also vanishes into thin air with our death. The passage between the parts of these three – equally existing – worlds takes place through our own body.

In Figure 1 I am trying to show how the non-imaginary words, i.e. the series of feelings of sounds, representing different parts of the external world are connected to the world around us through incoming feelings generated as a result of various interactions. The thick arrows symbolise that the words, or series of feelings of sounds, representing the external world form logical connections with each other within us.

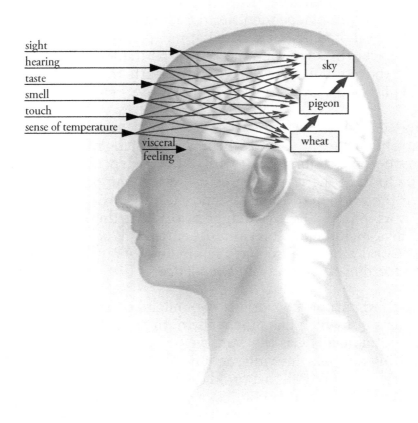

Figure 1

It is clear from the figure above that non-imaginary words of this type have external points of reference, or anchors, in the world around us. Therefore, these words mean the same in a relatively accurate way to everybody. And the results of the logical operations carried out with them can be easily checked in the external world.

What is the case with imaginary words? Do imaginary words have absolutely no connection with the external world? Do they have no points of reference or anchors? Well, the answer is complex. There are imaginary words that have connections and anchors, there are others that only have a few and there are others again that do not have any.

I am suggesting that we dig deeper into this issue. For the sake of simplicity, let us call our imaginary words simply notions. What is a notion? A notion is an imaginary word we create by putting parts of the world broken into pieces next to one another and examine the interactions they enter into. Then we only leave those parts in the group that have some specific characteristics we define or which meet the criteria we set up. Then we assign the same series of feelings of sound to each and every element of the remainder of the group.

Let us examine one particle of hydrogen, lithium and water for example. In the case of hydrogen and lithium, we can see that electrons orbit around a nucleus. But we can also see that the structure of the nucleuses and the number of the electrons are different in the two elements. In the case of water, the electrons orbit around a triple nucleus. Now we decide to assign the word 'atom' to every particle in which the electrons are orbiting around a single nucleus. And with this, we have created the notion of an atom which will cover the particles of several other materials.

As a matter of fact, there is no element called 'atom' in the periodic table. That is why the word 'atom' is a notion or an imaginary word. Look at Figure 2.

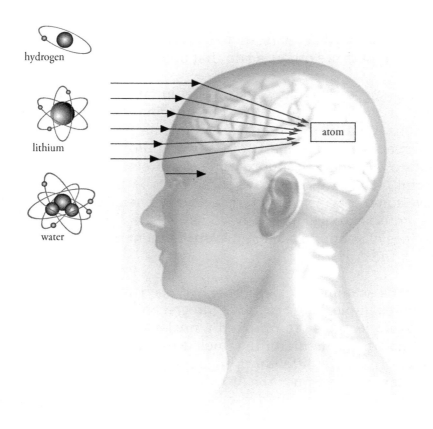

Figure 2

Now, in the same way, there is no hydrogen or lithium either as these words are also notions or imaginary words. Why? Because there are no two hydrogen atoms that are identical since at the same moment of time, the electron is in a different position relative to the nucleus in each and every hydrogen atom. So we assign the series of feelings of sound 'hydrogen' to a group of an endless number of particles that are actually different from one another and in which one electron orbits around one proton. And we have arrived back at the hopeless task of breaking up or cutting the world into pieces. Because, in theory, we should not assign one series of feelings of sound to two different things. But it would also be impossible to give a different name to each and every part of the universe. Therefore, as a matter of fact, almost every word we use is an imaginary word. An exception is some unique phenomena of the world that have proper names. Or so you may think. But actually, here the situation is even worse! Because we have forgotten about time that is maliciously laughing at our childish effort. Because no matter if we give the name X to something at a given moment of time, this something is going to change in a second and then, the next moment, we cannot call it X any more, only X' at best.

Due to the 'beneficial' contribution of time, each and every one of our non-imaginary words denotes things that do not exist in the external world: just like imaginary words do. In other words, we do not have one single word that would denote anything in the world around us. Tough, isn't it? The difference between the way imaginary words and non-imaginary words 'mean nothing' is that whereas we ourselves invent the phenomena denoted by imaginary words, we assign series of feelings of sounds to a part of the external world in the case of non-imaginary words, and this part disappears only because it gets transformed over the course of time.

Another important momentum is that while we have never had incoming feelings as a result of an interaction in connection with the phenomenon we invented in the case of an imaginary word, incoming feelings are indeed generated within us as a result of various interactions in the case of non-imaginary words. What is more: since our incoming feelings generated as a result of interactions are rather inaccurate – as we have seen previously – when we enter into an interaction with the part of the external world that changes slowly for us, we may perceive the given phenomenon as quasi-permanent. So, for example, if I take an apple in my hand and look at it thoroughly and then examine it again in an hour, I will not notice any change, so I will say that the apple is unchanged, which is, naturally, not true.

On this basis, we need to modify Figure 1 since – according to what we have just said – the words wheat, pigeon and sky are all imaginary words. Well, yes, they are but, in one way or another, they are still connected to the world around us.

Let us now see how notions are structured on the basis of their connection with the external world. I walk to a tree and I tear off three things. I have a look at them. All three have slightly different shapes and slightly different colours. I smell them and they smell relatively similar. Because of their different shape, they feel slightly different, too. Their taste is also slightly different: the ones that are greener are more sour. I shall call the first one X. Since the second one is similar to the first one, I shall call it X' and, by the same token, the third one X". Words created in this way are non-imaginary words because I assigned a non-repetitive and unique series of feelings of sound to one single piece of the external world. It is another issue that time does its job and in a second I would not be able to call them the same names since they would have already changed. In order not to waste my time with naming each thing on the tree and remembering all those names, based on my interactions with X, X' and X", I arbitrarily select the feelings of colour, shape and taste and, based on the similarity of those feelings across the things, I assign the series of feelings of sound 'Jonathan' to all of these things. The word 'Jonathan' is a notion, an imaginary word because Jonathan does not exist in the world around us. But this concept is connected to the world around us through a couple of arbitrarily selected incoming feelings.

I look around and notice that similar things – that are, however, substantially different from those on the first tree – grow on another tree. I also have a look at these: I smell them, I touch them and I taste them. I select three of them and I assign the series of feelings of sound Y, Y' and Y" to them. These words are non-imaginary words. However, time is passing… Then I assign the imaginary word 'Idared' to these non-imaginary words. This imaginary word is also connected to the external world with only a few incoming feelings (colour, shape, taste).

Fed up with tasting, smelling and touching, I decide to examine the things on the neighbouring trees only by looking at them and concentrating on shapes. I see long things, many tiny and regularly round things and things of all other possible shapes. Then I recognise that things very similar to the shapes of Jonathan and Idared grow on some of the trees. To these things, I assign the series of feelings of sound 'apple'. Of course, 'apple' is also a notion, an imaginary word. The notion apple is only connected to the world around us through my sight. This is, by the way, the level represented by the words wheat and pigeon in Figure 1. The imaginary word 'fruit' however, is not connected to the world around us through any incoming channel of feelings. What we assign the series of feelings of sound 'fruit' to is defined entirely by logical operations, not to mention the word 'crops' which is a notion of an even higher level than 'fruits'. Apart from the edible parts of plants, the word 'crops' can also be assigned to the propagation organs that we do not eat, such as grass seed, and also to the parts that can only be used for industrial purposes, such as cotton bolls. Moreover, you can sometimes use the word 'crops' for animals, for example when you talk about the pearls in a shell farm. Just like 'fruit', 'crops' is also an imaginary word that is not connected to the world around us through any incoming feelings. The imaginary words 'fruit' and 'crops' are defined by using other imaginary words and not feelings resulting from interactions with the external world.

Using all this as a starting point, we can draw the following conclusions:
- Different notions are connected to the external world through different amounts and qualities of incoming feelings.
- Built on one another, different notions constitute differ-

ent levels
- The higher the level a notion is at in the system, the fewer incoming feelings with which it is connected to the external world.
- Sometimes a given notion can get isolated from the external world so much that it is only defined using other notions.

Now let's look at Figure 3

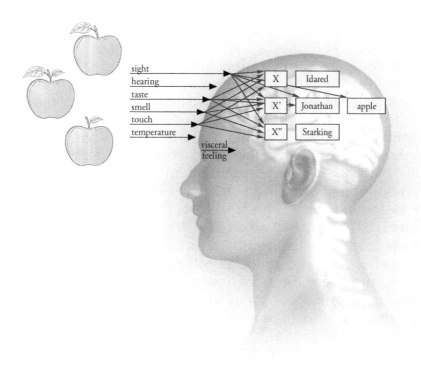

Figure 3

"Did I get it right?" My dear reader may ask "But then, what is the difference between the imaginary words used by sciences and human studies? How is it possible that the notions used by sciences are relatively accurate, whereas the words used by human studies are highly inaccurate?" The answer is simple. Sciences primarily use imaginary words

94

or notions there are connected to the external world with many incoming feelings, whereas human studies usually use words that often have no connections to the external world through incoming feelings at all.

In Figure 4, I show that the 'sterile' imaginary words used by human studies do not connect to the external world with the help of incoming feelings and there is nothing in the external world we could connect them to. More precisely, as the thin dotted arrows representing the incoming feelings of hearing show, the only thing these words have to do with in the external world is that we had to hear them at least once from another person, otherwise they would not be words at all.

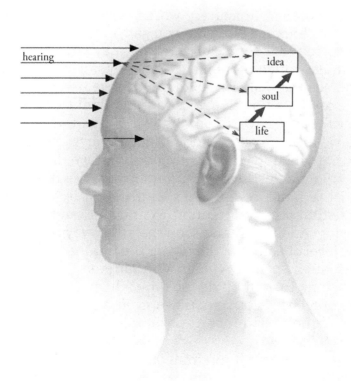

Figure 4
The thick arrows symbolise that the sterile imaginary

words may be in logical connections with one another. Or, to be more accurate, the sterile imaginary words, or series of feelings of sound, existing within us can only exist if they are in logical connection with one another because they define one another with the help of logical connections. They simply would not exist without logical connections since they do not have a direct point of reference in the external world. Let us take the imaginary word 'idea'. When we pronounce the series of feelings of sound 'idea', it just 'hangs in the air'. We need to explain it, we need to assign other words to it and need to put it into a system of logical connections in order to be able to interpret it. If I say 'sky', it is enough if you raise your eyes and stare into the endless blue of the sky.

Why do we need imaginary words, then? Because they speed up our thinking. But what you gain on the swings, you lose on the roundabouts. Our thinking may become much faster, but also much more inaccurate. If you look at Figure 3, you can see the higher level of notions we use, the larger pieces we are breaking the world around us into. However, the larger the pieces we break the world into, the more inaccurate we are. Of course, I do not mean physical size but the fact that while we are creating notions, we disregard a number of characteristics and interactions. The higher the level and the more comprehensive a notion is, the fewer characteristics we pay attention to and the fewer criteria we are using. And this is also true the other way round: the lower the level of a notion, the higher the number of criteria. As a consequence, many things with different characteristics can belong to a group denoted by a higher level notion based on only a few, or sometimes even only one, criteria. Just think of the word 'crops' for example.

In our mind, we can jump from one large, comprehensive notion to another much more easily than if we had to fill the space between these large notions with a long series of smaller and lower level notions. In other words, the thought "let us harvest the crops" can be thought in one second, whereas "Let us collect the Idared, Jonathan and Starking apples" takes a longer time. By using the latter sentence, however, we can avoid harvesting the crops of angel's trumpet (Datura stramonium) which contain deadly poison.

When we examine the world around us, we can carry out the cutting up of the external world and the assigning of words, i.e. series of feelings of sound, to the pieces relatively accurately. Moreover, this accuracy is increasing with the development of science. But what is the case with the accuracy of sterile imaginary words used by human studies? With words such as idea, wholeness, spirit, necessary, virtue, truth, good, bad, perfect, value, homeland, freedom, democracy, economy and so on. How accurate are these words? They are exactly as accurate as the other words defining them are. In other words, the accuracy of a sterile imaginary word depends on the accuracy of the words defining it. The errors of definitions of words, however, accumulate or even multiply. This is why the accuracy of the imaginary words in human studies deteriorates at a highly increased rate. Because a word defined by a sterile, high-level notion will be even less accurately defined than the original notion defining it, not to mention the words to be defined by our newly defined word.

In the case of imaginary words that are connected to the external world with many incoming feelings, the inaccuracy of a word comes from the inaccuracy of cutting the world into pieces and from the deviation or inaccuracy of our feelings. These are the words sciences tend to use. There are, however, imaginary words defined with other imaginary words also in sciences and the potential for increased inaccuracy is there but we always have the opportunity to check the accuracy of our definition in the external world. At the end of a logical sequence, we can carry out an experiment in the external world through which we can get feedback, and if we got something wrong, we can correct it. That is why engineers can create aeroplanes and politicians or economists cannot govern countries.

To simplify matters and make them easier to understand, in the following chapters I will use the expressions 'imaginary world' and 'imaginary word' exclusively for words that do not have any connections with the external world, i.e. for sterile imaginary words. And now let us get back to the level of the science of feelings because that is where the rub is.

9.

THE MIXING BOWL

The 13th floor, the level of feelings, has a particular importance because this is the level where feelings relating to the world around us and feelings relating to the imaginary world separate, or mix, for us. "What mixing? What is this guy talking about?" the dear reader may ask. The mess is caused by the fact that our brain handles well-defined and undefined words in the same way. For our brains, both categories of words are series of feelings of sound which our brain treats equally, without making any difference between them. This makes me think of the joke about the electrician teaching his apprentice: "You know, son, a live wire looks exactly the same as a dead wire. Only the touch is different." Well, accurately defined words also look the same as inaccurately defined words, only the use of them yields different results.

At the level of series of feelings of sound, our brain works like the builder in the beginning of this book who is trying to build a castle without differentiating between building blocks made of stone and those made of ice. No matter whether he applies the strictest logical principles and no matter how precisely he fits his building blocks, when warm weather comes, it will all collapse anyway.

Let me emphasise once more that I do not have any personal problem with the great thinkers of the past. They did what they had to do and what they could do. We need to see, however, that they were trying to explain our world from top to bottom. They were trying to explain with inaccurate imaginary words the external world that can only be described with highly accurate non-imaginary words. It is similar to trying to carve a microprocessor with a stone axe. It does not usually work out.

Let us now go back a little to the problem of changing dimensions and to the story of the lady who has been cheated on. Reading the first part of her account, we see that she is using words which are connected to feelings coming from interactions with the external world, words that describe the world around her, for her. These words symbolise bits of the external world: cat, door, bed etc. If we want, we can define these words pretty accurately with the help of the science of physics, chemistry or biology. In the second part of her account, the lady changes dimensions and moves to an imaginary world. She starts using words, or rather notions, which do not denote any of the parts of the external world and, therefore, do not have a point of reference: morals, faith, guilt, wealth. We cannot directly describe these words with the help of either physics or chemistry or biology. How could we possibly describe the word 'morals' with the help of physics? Or what could chemistry do with the word 'faith'? Nothing, absolutely nothing.

Getting back to the story of the lady, what did actually happen there? When the lady caught the husband with their neighbour's wife, she tried to interpret what had happened. She tried but she failed because how could she interpret what had happened at the level of biology, chemistry or physics? No way. No one else could have done so either. Why not? Because a level was missing: the level of the science of feelings. The events of her story took place at the level of the science of feelings and therefore, they give us an interpretable picture at this same level and not at the level of biology, chemistry or physics. At levels below the level of the science of feelings, we can only recognise fragments of the picture or minor circumstances. In order to have a comprehensive and interpretable picture, we need to move further up and look at the events from a higher perspective, from above, if you like. The events of the story of the lady can be described and interpreted most easily with the science of feelings. It is a different issue whether you can further analyse the feelings participating in the process at the levels of neurobiology, biology, chemistry and physics. Not knowing the level of the science of feelings, and not being able to make any use of biology, chemistry and physics, the lady, for want of a better idea, escaped to the imaginary world, changed dimensions and described the events with imaginary words.

The lady will implement the faulty results of her decisions made in the imaginary world in real life, and all the participants in her story will suffer from the consequences. And it is not only this particular lady: billions of people commit the same mistake every day. The fact that Uncle Joe, sitting in the pub and discussing the philosophical questions of life, draws wrong conclusions is acceptable. That is the way it is. It is not a tragedy either that philosophers in their ivory towers built beautifully ornamented castles in the air from imaginary words. But when heads of states make decisions and make the lives of millions miserable is not so funny. One does not feel like laughing so much.

As a consequence of Hitler's wrong decisions drawn from logical operations made with imaginary words like 'übermensch', 'lebensraum' and 'ruling the world' 50 million people died, not to mention 'smaller scale' massacres such as the Inquisition, or various religious wars. Logical operations made with poorly defined imaginary words can be incredibly dangerous. "Then what shall we do instead?" my dear reader may ask. "Must we throw away all the imaginary words and notions and never use them again?" Well, we need to put them in order, that is for sure. Some words we must throw away because they only cause confusion, while others we must reinterpret or, in other words, ground. What? Ground words? Yes, in some way or another, we need to make them connected to the external world.

10.

GROUNDING

Yes, imaginary words must be grounded. Just as they do with multi-storey buildings. When they build the electrical network on each of the floors of a multi-storey building, they connect the equipment on each floor with the earth wire to ground it, that is, they connect the earth wire to the earth wire of the floor below, which they connect to the floor below that and so on, down to the ground. They do not connect earth wires to the earth wire of the floor above because then the network would never be grounded; only skied, at best. But we need to ground things.

Many philosophers and thinkers of the past committed exactly this mistake: they did not ground words, they skied them. In other words, instead of trying to connect the words to the world around us, they did the exact opposite: they tried to connect those words to the sky of the imaginary world of ideas. But we need to ground things.

Can you imagine a situation where you have to ground the 14th floor but the 14th floor is hanging in the air because there is no 13th floor below it? Could you do it? I have my doubts. However, that is exactly the situation with humankind: the imaginary dimension simply cannot be grounded.

It cannot be connected to the world of biology, chemistry and physics that explores the external world because the science of the level of feelings – the world of undiscovered, hushed up and forbidden feelings - is missing.

But why are feelings so crucial? Because there is only one world that exists for the individual and that is the world of feelings! The external world, just like our internal world and our thoughts – which are nothing else but the combined series of feelings of sound – all appear in us in the form of feelings. Simply there is no other world for the individual. When we are completely convinced that we are examining the world around us – for example how blue the sky is, how wonderful a glass of wine tastes or how pretty Julie is – what we are actually examining is nothing but our own feelings. And this is the very same world, the world of feelings, that we did not want to examine! Do we not want to examine the **WORLD**? It is complete and utter nonsense to understand ourselves and the world around us without examining the world of feelings. It simply does not work. It is impossible. **Therefore, the primary task of humankind is to explore the world of feelings.** We do not need to fidget with stars or fiddle about in the world of subatomic particles. We must not spend billions on things whose time has not yet come. Do you think starvation, poverty and wars will disappear from the earth if we discover more galaxies or a couple of new miserable particles?

Imagine a married couple with two kids who are shipwrecked and get washed up on the shores of a desert island. The two unfortunate kids are standing there soaking wet, shaking with cold and exhausted. Mummy and Daddy though, instead of trying to light a fire that would warm them up or trying to find shelter or putting together a hut, instead of looking for food and drinking water for their kids and for themselves, just lie down on the sand and start staring at the stars:

"Darling! Look, how beautifully the Alpha Centauri is shining. How far do think it is from us?"

"Oh darling! It must be 1.338 parsec, or about 4.365 light years, from us. It is shining so beautifully because its spectrum type is G2V/K1V and its absolute brightness is 4.38/5.71."

What would you say to a story like that? You would definitely say, without hesitation, that they need immediate help, and medical help, for that matter, psychiatric help, to be precise, and possibly in an institution. Actually humankind is acting out exactly the same story but on a much larger scale. And to make it more interesting, we also slaughter each other in local wars. Should we not rather concentrate on the only world that exists for the individual? Should we not explore this world to prevent starvation and to avoid killing each other? Is space research important? Yes, it is. Is particle physics important? Yes, it is but only after we have put things in order in our minds. Of course, we can also bury our heads in the sand and pretend that we are dumb but that usually does not bring fruit. So let us move on and have a look at Figure 5

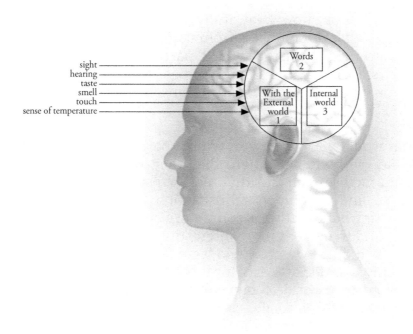

Figure 5

Figure 5 shows the WORLD, the only world that exists for the individual. I suggest dividing the huge sea of feelings that exist in the individual into 3 groups. This is, of course, an arbitrary step that only serves the purpose of better understanding. As a matter of fact, these parts constitute a close and indivisible unity within us.

The first group represents the feelings generated by direct interactions with the external world. The feelings include the senses of sight, hearing, smell, taste, touch and temperature, and also some of the visceral feelings which help us sense our spatial position through gravity. This is the group that is the most 'tangible' for today's people.

The second group is the group of words, i.e. series of feelings of sound that provide the basis for thinking in symbols. And it is a new idea for many that words are also feelings.

The third group is the group of feelings resulting from interactions within our internal world. This is the naughty, confused, sinful, amoral and disgusting world dealing with which has been considered a sin until now. I think, however, it is worth devoting a couple of sentences to this hushed up and despised group. First, I said "feelings resulting from interactions within our internal world". Some of my readers may ask the question "What is interacting with what in our internal world? Or is it we ourselves that interact with our own internal world? How can you interact with yourself?" The difficulties of interpreting this sentence are caused by the fact that we are accustomed to looking at ourselves as an indivisible whole. But this is not the case at all. Our body consists of different organs made up of billions of cells. So there are interactions taking place within us human beings, and what is more, these interactions make it possible for us to live. As I mentioned, the special characteristic of this group of feelings is that they are generated on the basis of interactions within us human beings, and their generation is not in direct connection with interactions with the external world. The most graphic examples of these feelings are hunger and thirst. We become hungry and thirsty even if we are sitting on the couch not doing anything. These two feelings appear in us as a result of processes and interactions taking place in our organism. But the same applies to other need-indicating, strategic, tactical, technological and status-indicating feelings. For example, we can only desire an apple if we see it (let us now disregard the special case of recalling eating apples from our memory), although the feeling of desire has nothing, absolutely nothing, to do with the apple existing in the external world. Desire is created as a result of an interaction between the centre of desire and the centre of sight that shows us the image of the apple and not as a result of an interaction between the centre of desire and the apple. Our centre of desire does not even know about the existence of the apple: for this centre, the apple does not exist at all, it is only interacting with the feelings appearing in the centre of sight in our internal world.

Another important fact we need to pay attention to is that feelings – and this is true for all the three groups – are mostly responsible for one thing and that is to make it possible for us to adapt to the external world. This statement I should support with a more detailed explanation, but for the moment, I ask the dear reader to take my word for it (I discussed the issue in detail in my book *Feelings*). We can consider the feelings of the first group as a channel that is responsible for sending the results of different interactions to the CPU (Central Processing Unit) where the data is actually processed. The CPU sends control signals, in the forms of feelings, that form the third group. It is primarily the feelings of this third group that help us to adapt to the external world.

"And what is the case with thinking? Is it not thinking that helps us to adapt to the environment?" my dear reader may ask. Let us not forget that thinking in words developed later both in ontogeny and phylogeny, so we were able to exist without thinking in words, that is series of feelings of sound, but we were not able to exist without the feelings of the third group! If we adapt to the external world primarily on the basis of the feelings of the third group, then it is exactly these feelings that define our attitude to the external world and our reactions in a certain situations. In other words, these feelings define the behaviour of Joseph, Kathleen or Steve, they define what kinds of traits they have and what sorts of people they are. So, should we skip the examination of these feelings?

Today, humankind has reached the stage of examining only one of these three groups in detail: the feelings resulting from direct interactions with the external world. We have had some achievements in examining words or series of feelings of sound but we did it in a rather special way: we focused our attention on the systematisation of these words and on the rules of using them. The examination of feelings of the third group, i.e. feelings resulting from internal interactions, practically does not exist. Dear psychologist readers, I have bad news for you. The science of psychology will not be able to take a single step ahead without examining the third group of feelings. It is simply impossible. You will make no progress and you will struggle with nonsensical theories, all in vain: you will be massaging air. You cannot skip the 13th floor. Believe me. If you do not start some comprehensive and detailed research into feelings, you are only wasting your time and, even worse, you are wasting the time of humankind as well, while billions of people live in physical or mental need or both.

Taking all this into consideration, let us now try to have a look at the process science is currently using to explore and understand feelings resulting from interactions with the external world, i.e. the first group of feelings in Figure 5.

My eyes are closed. My outstretched hand knocks against something. A feeling of cold appears in me. I am touching the thing and a feeling of hardness appears in me. I open my eyes and a 'feeling of image' appears in me. See Figure 6. (Although it is not particularly important for the topic of this book, we still need to point out that the expression 'feeling of image' is a bit of a misinterpretation. During its evolution, the sense of sight probably developed from feelings but it has already outgrown the notion of feeling. It is now a nervous activity of much higher data traffic and bandwidth which, in terms of function, can be classified as a sense).

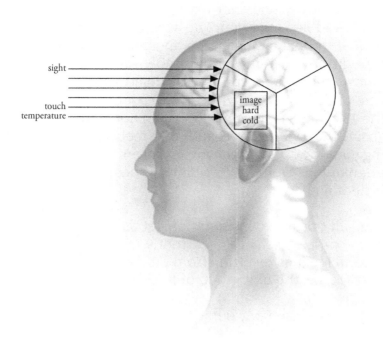

Figure 6

Now I assign series of feelings of sound to the feelings appearing in me, that is, I am creating words. See Figure 7.

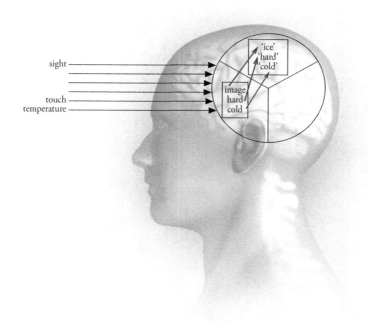

Figure 7

Attention! The feelings shown in Figure 7 are all feelings and not the external world. They are just as legitimate feelings as the need-indicating, orienting, strategic, tactical and technological feelings shown below in Figure 8. And the feelings shown in the third group of Figure 8 are just as real as the feelings shown in the first and second groups. They are not a tiny bit less valuable or inferior and they are neither sinful, nor disgusting nor detestable.

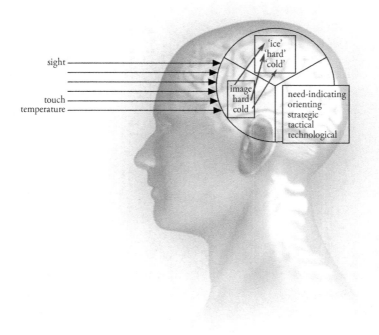

Figure 8

What is today's psychology doing? It is using exactly the method shown in Figure 7: looking at the individual from an external point of view. Psychologists expose the subjects of their experiments to different interactions and influences and check what kind of reactions those interactions and influences trigger in those subjects. (See Figure 9 below).

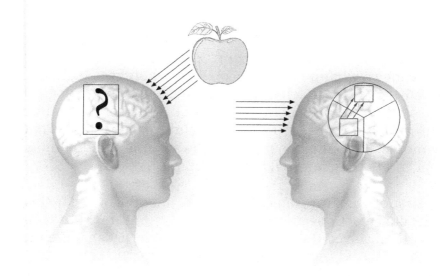

Figure 9

More precisely, what they are examining is the reactions and activities controlled by the third group of feelings in their subjects. Psychologists are trying to draw conclusions about something from these reactions. Something, because, as a matter of fact, they do not know what they are examining. They are not aware that they are examining reactions controlled by the third group of feelings. And as a consequence, they are also not aware that they should actually find out the secrets of the feelings of third group because it is the feelings of the third group that control the reactions they trigger, that is it is this group of feelings that governs and controls us human beings. Instead, they skip the level of feelings, the 13th floor, and try to do something on the level of biology and biochemistry and, naturally, fail to do so. Instead of simply knocking on the door of the third group of feelings, saying hello and having a look around. Yes, I know there was a period in psychology that was based on introspection or self-observation, however, this method was not considered objective enough as there is only one person who can do the observation and see the results, and they declared that these results were too subjective for external observers because who knows what another person

117

feels. And that is quite right: who knows? But it is true for all the feelings shown in Figure 8! Oops! In other words: who knows what another person feels when he sees, hears, smells, tastes or touches something? So it is quite illogical to say that the perspective of an external observer is more objective than the perspective of an internal observer. What is more, external examination is always much-much more inaccurate than internal examination.

First of all, during an external examination, one can only examine reactions triggered by feelings and not the feelings themselves that control the reactions. This is already a transfer. And sometimes many feelings participate in triggering the reaction. It is easy to misunderstand a given reaction if you don't understand the mechanism of interactions between the feelings behind it.

Second, in the case of an internal examination, you need to be prepared for accumulated errors and distortions. It starts with the physical distortion of the transmission medium interacting with the person under examination, the limits and inaccuracy of the threshold level, spectrum, dynamics and chronology of the interaction and the interference with other feelings of the person under examination which is only doubled by the same errors and distortions in the scientist carrying out the experiment which also influence the results.

And third, psychologists do not connect the results of external examinations to feelings triggered in the subject of the experiment. They do not examine what feelings triggered those reactions. They do not examine exactly what they should be examining. It is true, they cannot because they are not aware of the feelings that control and govern our reactions and activities. The operation was successful, only the patient died.

In modern day psychology, beautifully complex theories are made up with the use of ungrounded and undefined imaginary words such as 'conscious', 'subconscious', 'psyche' etc. This, however, leads one to become isolated from the external world and to commit mistakes. As for the subjectivity of internal examination: it is obvious, but any examination focused on the external world is just a subjective one. The misconception that the external world we experience is more objective than our internal feelings comes from the fact that people identify the external world they experience with the real external world. But the real external world that exists independent of us is relative. Let us not forget that the quality of the external world depends on who is examining it and what interactions take place between examiner and subject. In us, the external world appears through feelings generated during interactions, feelings that are just as subjective as any other internal feelings of ours including need-indicating, orienting, strategic, tactical and technological feelings.

Of course, our subjectivity works within well-defined limits. Based on the high level of similarity between the structure of the nervous system and the chemical processes taking place in our organism, we reasonably suppose that we react to a given interaction within certain limits or extreme values. The differences between reactions can be predicted with more or less accuracy according to our internal makeup. In simpler terms, we are subjective or individual only within an easily predictable tolerance. As a consequence, the tolerance and accuracy of the results of our internal examinations can also be predicted and objectivised in exactly the same way predefined levels of tolerance are applied in measurements in technical sciences. Yes, you can do it. You can immerse yourself in your internal world.

There are people who categorically declare that it is impossible to explore our feelings. Let me answer this suggestion with a well-known bon mot: "Everybody knows that certain things cannot be done until somebody turns up who has not heard about it and does it." Yes, indeed, you can learn how to explore feelings. The emphasis is on learning: you can learn how to do it the same way you learn how to see. Some of my readers, I suppose, are looking a little puzzled, thinking what nonsense it is. What do you mean, you learn how to see? Everybody can see. Yes it is true: everybody can see. Once they've learned how to do it. Because newborns do not yet see, or rather, the light interacts with the nerve endings in their eyes but they cannot differentiate shapes.

Of course, there may be more talented and less talented people also in the field of exploring feelings. If you are not too good at it, you had better not become a psychologist. Not everyone can become a pilot either. The important thing is to concentrate on your actual feelings and not on what you think you should feel. First, choose one feeling out of the ocean of feelings and then, after you have focused your attention on it and have more or less isolated it, start considering what you felt, not the other way round.

Since we have apparently diverged from the topic of grounding imaginary words, I suggest we get back to it. Thinking with words is the more accurate the fewer imaginary words we use or – if we need to use imaginary words – the more anchors our imaginary words are connected to the external world with. 'Earth-bound thinking' has a slightly pejorative connotation but this is the real deal. That is what we need. I can imagine that some of my readers are pursing their lips. You shouldn't. Go to the mirror and check how much nicer you look with a smile on your face. Physicians, chemists and biologists all use 'earth-bound' thinking, whereas the proponents of human studies soar and look down with contempt on the researchers of sciences messing about with clods. Ironically, however, while the aeroplanes made by natural scientists messing about with clods fly in the air, the flying carpet of the proponents of those soaring human studies lies in the dust due to weaving errors. And it will be so until the proponents of human studies learn how to mess about with clods. You bet.

If we want to ground or anchor a sterile imaginary word, if we want to connect it to the external world, we can choose the following options or even a combination:

1. We assign the given word to our incoming feelings.
2. We assign this word to another sterile imaginary word (this solution does not usually work).
3. We assign the word to an already grounded or anchored word.
4. We assign the word to a feeling of the third group of feelings coming from our internal world.

There are no further options. There are no options 5, 6 or 7. We must simply get on with it.

In order to understand the process of grounding in practice, let me invite you on an imaginary journey. I suggest travelling to the rainforests of the Amazon where it is always raining and trees grow so densely and so tall that you cannot even see the sky. We ask the first indigenous person who comes our way if she knows what the word '*grrhuss*' means. Of course, our native friend will look puzzled because this word does not exist in the local language. Although this word is not an imaginary word because it represents a very specific part of the world, from the subjective point of view of our native friend, this word behaves like an imaginary word because it has not yet been grounded, it has not yet been anchored in her mind: it is not connected to the external world. Let us then try and help her understand, ground and anchor this word. Let us try method 2. Let us tell her that '*grrhuss*' is something that has two '*grrtuktuks*', a '*spuri*' and some '*zikzaks*'. After saying this sentence we will see that our native friend is staring at us like a stuck pig. This is completely natural, however, because we were trying to define the word that is undefined for her with other words that are also undefined for her, that is they are not connected to the external world. We committed exactly the same mistake billions of people commit every day.

Okay, I think it is clear now that this method does not work so now we ask our friend to come along so we can show her the *grrhuss*. This is nothing else but the application of method 1. As soon as we arrive at the *grrhuss*, our friend can walk around it, have a proper look at it, touch it and smell it. We can even startle it so our friend can hear what kind of noise it makes. Now the *grrhuss* has been transformed in our friend's mind. It is not an imaginary word any more, it is a series of feelings of sound assigned to one particular part of the external world with the help of feelings. This process of grounding is shown in Figure 10.

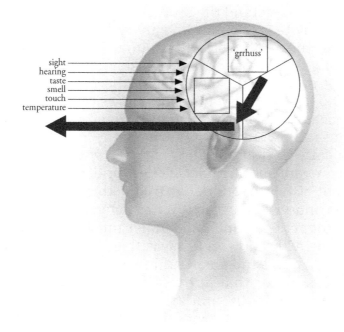

Figure 10

Figure 10 is exactly the same as Figure 7 only in the reverse direction. In Figure 7 we created a word on the basis of interactions with the external world, whereas in this case, we connected an existing series of feelings of sound to feelings generated in us as a result of interactions with the external world.

Of course, we would not have had to use imaginary words, because our native friend does not speak English either so we could have told her it was an aeroplane with two engines, a landing gear and some stabilisers. But this way probably my readers could better imagine themselves in the position of the native person. After she has walked around the aeroplane several times, she is still very interested in what the *grrhuss* might be, in other words, what it is good for and in what ways it can interact with the external world. And with this, we have arrived at a very important question, namely the depth of grounding. How deep, and in how much detail, should we ground a given sterile imaginary word? Because this is the moment when our native friend comes up with an endless line of 'Why and How' questions. "Why does it take off? In what conditions is lifting power generated on the surface of objects moving against air? What is air? What is a molecule? What is an atom? What is a subatomic particle?" and so on. This is a natural process since if I interact with something – I look at it, I smell it, I touch it or I listen to it –questions may arise about what it is we are interacting with, what other things does it interact with and how do those other things interact with yet other things and so on till the end of days. There is no way to stop anymore. The deeper we dig in the chain of interactions, naturally, the more comprehensive the picture we get about the external world, the better we ground the given word and the deeper our anchor is buried into the soil of the real world. The levels of biology, chemistry and physics offer deeper and deeper grounding and bury their anchor in more and more soil.

So how deeply should you ground words? It depends on a number of factors: your capacity, your education, your interest, the given situation and so on. Talking about the depth of grounding words, when do you think a word is completely grounded? The short answer is: never. The long answer is also never, only with a few more words. How could we ground the entire world? If we created the complete image of the entire world in our mind. Or in other words, if we could make an image of each and every part of the external world and each and every interaction of each and every part in our minds. This sounds rather hopeless. All we can do is to depict the part of the world we are examining together with its interactions as much as we feel necessary at a given moment. Our efforts to ground an imaginary word are aimed at assigning the given series of feelings of sound to other feelings (they may also be series of feelings of sound) with the help of which we can integrate it into the system of feelings that have been generated in us while we were depicting the external world. But let us move on.

For our grounding effort, we can also use method 3 which assigns already grounded or anchored words to the word '*grrhuss*'. We can tell a friend that the *grrhuss* looks like a huge bird with open wings, that it is made of a heavy and hard material which shines like silver, that it has a strange, slightly pungent smell and it roars loudly if you start it. The words huge, bird, wing, heavy, hard, silver, pungent and roar are all lower level notions – and not imaginary words – which are already grounded and anchored to the external world with the help of our feelings. Naturally, these more or less grounded words cannot replace the feelings experienced during the interaction with the *grrhuss* in method 1 but they can still give you some clues and connect the series of feelings of sound *grrhuss* to the external world to some extent. 'Why and How' questions will also be asked when using method 3. Whereas in the case of using method 1, we should have disassembled the aeroplane into small bits and pieces to have a look at, touch, smell and tap each and every piece in order to be able to answer these questions, when using method 3, we can avoid disassembly. We can replace the disassembling of the aeroplane by describing the machinery with more or less grounded technical words, for example wing, propeller, engine, shaft, spring, lubricant, fuel etc. When we want to ground a notion with the help of method 3, we need to do it in multiple steps. In such a case, there is no other choice but to trace the original word back to increasingly precisely defined and more grounded words moving down gradually through the levels of notions the same way we showed in Figure 3, only in the opposite direction. The difficulty of the processes is that, although the number of interactions the smaller and smaller pieces can have gradually decreases, the larger pieces consist of such a high number of variations of smaller pieces that it is sometimes almost incomprehensible for a human being.

This is exactly what the sciences of biology, chemistry and physics deal with. All these sciences do is break the world into small pieces and assign series of feelings of sound to the small pieces, i.e. create words, give the small pieces a name and then examine what interactions the newly formed and named pieces have with other pieces.

A consequence of the above paragraphs is this: as we try to ground a word by using method 3, that is moving from less defined notions to lower level and more defined notions, we will eventually come to a point where there are no such lower level notions or, in other words, where science – while cutting the world into pieces in the given field – has not yet reached the level of offering us the piece, the notion or the word we need. Without words we cannot use method 3 since we cannot think in the absence of the necessary notions and words: we cannot carry out operations with things that do not exist.

Of course, you may think that this is all bullshit as everything in science is measured with different instruments and human feelings do not play a role. What could instruments have to do with human feelings? An instrument is objective, whereas feelings are subjective. This is a perfectly understandable thought. And yet... The most important thing is that sciences do not break the external world into pieces, only the image of the external world generated in scientists through various interactions. They break the image of the world, i.e. the world of feelings, into pieces. Or rather, images of the world because there are many many worlds like that: exactly as many as there are people living in the world.

So the world we are examining is not the external world, only an image of it depicted by our feelings generated in series of interactions. We are in the same place again: nothing else exists for us human beings apart from the world of our own feelings. This statement however has important consequences. When we think that we are cutting the world into pieces we're doing nothing else but cutting up feelings resulting from interactions with the external world and when we think that we are examining interactions between the various parts of the existing world, what we are actually doing is examining interactions between the pieces of our feelings. Let us not forget, however, that these pieces of feelings are not independent of the external world! These feelings are generated in us through interactions so they are connected to the external world through interactions. Therefore, if we want to depict the external world, we cannot connect these feelings in a random way and we cannot vary them as we please.

On the subject of the instruments' objectivity and our subjectivity, the answer is simpler than you may think at first sight. If I am watching Pamela who is standing 100 metres away from me, I am actually not interacting with Pamela at all but with the transmission medium, light, that Pamela has modulated with her characteristic features. When I hear Pamela shouting, I am not interacting with Pamela but with the transmission medium, air which, again, Pamela has modulated with her characteristic features. What happens if I produce a telescope in order to see Pamela better and what happens if I produce a radio to hear Pamela better?
"Grandma, why do you have such big eyes?"

"So that I can see you better."

"Oh, Grandma, and why do you have such big ears?"

"So that I can hear you better."

"Oh, Grandma, and why do you have such a big mouth?"

"..."

When we use an instrument we do nothing else but introduce another transmission medium, or possibly even a complete chain of transmission media for that matter. And we can play as we please with this chain of transmission media: we can strengthen or weaken the original interaction if we need to, we can make it perceivable for ourselves and so on and so forth. The outcome at the end, however, will be the same. At the end of the whole performance someone will have to read the meters and the readings will appear as feelings in our world of images, so we still cannot avoid our subjectivity.

But let us move on and look at method 4. Does it make any sense in the given case to assign the series of feelings of sound '*grrhuss*' to the feelings of the third group coming from our internal world? Of course not. The thing you want to assign the series of feelings of sound '*grrhuss*' to exists in the external world and not in us: no aeroplanes fly in our heads.

Before trying to ground a sterile imaginary word, we need to examine whether that particular thing can be connected to the external world or rather to our internal world. In other words, we need to decide if we should start searching in our internal world or in the external world. Naturally, there may be words that strongly connect to both the external world and our internal world and during the grounding of which we need to take both paths. Just as we did before. You remember, since we have grounded an imaginary word together. What was it? It was the word 'word'. When we were defining the meaning of the term 'word' we did nothing else but ground or anchor the notion of 'word'. According to the traditional definition: "word is the smallest meaningful unit of a language". In this definition, the notion of 'word' is defined by other sterile imaginary words such as language and meaning. How can the word 'meaning' define anything if the word 'meaning' is not yet defined either? But we solved the problem and defined the word 'word' by anchoring it to the world around us through our incoming feelings and to our internal non-imaginary world through other feelings. So we took both paths.

And what is the case with imaginary words like love or morals. How could we ground these words? Well, some of you may have guessed. Yes, through the nasty, detestable, disgusting and guilty third group of feelings. (Take a look at Figure 11.)

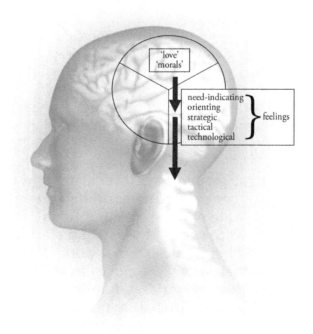

Figure 11

Why? The answer is simple: because there is nothing

in the external world we could connect these words to. No morals with a strict look on their faces walk in the streets. So method 1, which is based on the use of incoming feelings, does not work in this case. Therefore, as we cannot start in the direction of the external world, we can only start searching in our own internal world. Although these words are connected to the external world but their connection is us, ourselves. So these words can only be grounded through us, through our internal world or, to be more precise, through our body. Why? Because our body is a part of the world, and it is our body that makes it possible for feelings to be generated within us. Our body is the link, the passage between the external world, the mapped world and the imaginary world. But let us move one step further. For the sake of simplicity, we can also exclude method 2. Now, let us look at method 3, the method of grounded words. But we cannot see it. The words humankind has been using until today to describe feelings are completely inaccurate. They are only series of feelings of sound about which it impossible to tell what they are assigned to. If we dig deeper, we will see that these words mostly describe undefined and inaccurate fragments of feeling formations the parts of which, and the connections of those parts, are completely unknown.

The fact that humankind has not yet dealt with the world of feelings, and has neglected the 13th floor, means we have not yet cut the third group of feelings generated during the interactions of our internal world into pieces, and therefore, naturally we could not have examined the interactions between them either. And, of course, if we have not done the cutting, we could not have assigned series of feelings of sound to the pieces, so we could not have created the necessary words either. So we cannot think about the third group of feelings, arising from the interactions of our internal world, because we do not have the words to do so, not to mention grounding where we would need notions of different levels and the connections between them in order to be able to use method 3.

And this is where I would like to mention my book *Feelings* again. My book gives a detailed overview of the world of our feelings, it breaks the groups of feelings into pieces and names those pieces, i.e. creates new words, explores the interactions between the pieces and models and describes individual behaviour based on those interactions. Naturally, my book cannot replace the years of persistent research of hundreds of scientists, it can only give guidance in terms of which direction to take. I am confident, however, that I have succeeded in finding some connections based on which we can move forward in the exploration of our feelings and also in interpreting and grounding words.

I know I should now illustrate with a couple of examples how we can ground a sterile imaginary word, for example 'morals', using the method I created. I would suggest coming back to this issue at the end of the book when my dear reader will have acquired the necessary knowledge and will have understood the interactions and connections between different types of feelings. And now let us learn about method 4, in which a sterile imaginary word is assigned to a feeling of the third group of feelings, those originating from our internal world. In order to better understand the process, it helps if we approach things from the other side. (Look at Figure 12)

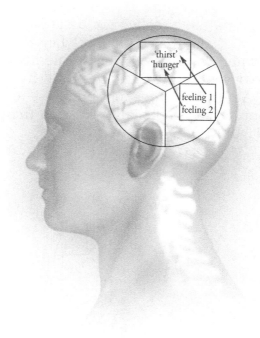

Figure 12

Figure 12 shows how we create words and how we assign series of feelings of sound to feelings of the third group, which originate in our internal world. Sometimes it is a relatively simple process. If the feeling we are experiencing is a characteristic feeling of high-intensity that can be easily separated from its environment, we have an easy job, we can easily create pieces and we can easily assign series of feelings of sound to those pieces of feelings.

The situation is a lot more complicated when we talk about low intensity or short feelings or even parallel or composite feelings or their combinations, not to mention feelings that serve different purposes but share similar qualities. That is why it is so difficult to cut or break the third group of feelings, originating in our internal world, into pieces.

In the case shown in Figure 12, we have a relatively easy job. If we can separate a feeling, we assign a series of feelings of sound to it and that is all. But when the direction is the reverse, when we have a given sterile imaginary word such as the series of feelings of sound 'love', it is much more complicated. A plethora of feelings are present in us at any given moment. Which one shall we assign the given word to? (Look at Figure 13)

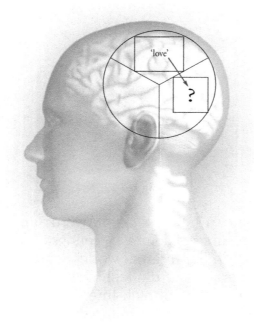

Figure 13

Nothing is more simple, my dear reader may think, let us just do the same thing we did when we took our indigenous friend to the aeroplane. Let us put a nice little bird, a kitten, a puppy or a sweet little baby into her hands and let us tell her love is what she is feeling now. If you are lucky, this method may work but it is not at all certain it will work for everyone. First, although everyone needs love, love is not present in everyone every time. Second, in a given moment, many feelings are present in one person. How can you select the feeling of love out of all those feelings, supposing the feeling of love is really present in the same moment, that is? Remember that our native friend had a relatively easy job when we were showing her the aeroplane. The first groups of feelings originating from her interactions with the external world had already been broken into pieces. That is, when she saw the world around her she could differentiate between trees, the airport building, us and the aeroplane. Although she was hearing the chirp of the birds, our voice and the sound of the aeroplane at the same time, she could separate them and she knew what to assign those sounds to. She was feeling the smell of the jungle, our perfume and the smell of the kerosene, but she could separate all those different smells and she knew what to assign to those smells.

The fact that the feelings of the first group that are generated in our interactions with the external world are cut into pieces, i.e. they are classified, seems obvious and natural to us adults. But all of us have come through the period of breaking up and classifying these feelings when we were babies. For a baby, the feelings originating from the interactions with the external world form a uniform mass. The world of the baby has not yet been broken up. Light interacts with his eyes, but he cannot differentiate between shapes and objects. He can hear sounds because the air makes his eardrums vibrate but he cannot connect those sounds to anything. For an average person, the third group of feelings – the feelings generated in internal interactions – is not yet broken up or classified. If we tried to show someone what love is without a verbal explanation, we would be in the same position as if we had tried to show the aeroplane to our native friend when she was still a baby. The average mortal has not learned how to differentiate between feelings of the third group. Exceptions to this rule are some very strong and distinct feelings such as hunger, thirst, tiredness or pain. For most of us, however, the world of the feelings generated in internal interactions is a lost world, an ever-changing mass of confusion which hardly ever comes to the surface. Of course, we should not forget about the fact that these feelings are still feelings just like the ones in the first group generated in interactions with the external world or the ones in the second group that are series of feelings of sound. The third group can also be broken or cut into pieces and the interactions between them can also be explored. We can understand this part of the world.

Getting back to grounding the series of feelings of sound 'love' with method 4, we must face the fact that this problem cannot be solved right away. If we do not break the feelings of the third group into pieces and do not explore the connections between them, we have no chance of grounding the sterile imaginary word 'love' and assigning it to any of the millions of feelings. Today's reality supports this claim. People do not really know what the series of feelings of sound 'love' stands for. We encounter this word day by day from dawn to dusk. We read it in literary works or in the press; we hear it in movies, on the radio or on television. Its importance is emphasised everywhere and everyone is called on to love everyone else, only they forget to tell us what love actually is. The word 'love' just hangs in the air. It is a nice but rather vague something. I can love Julie, my parents, my children, my neighbour, my dog, my cat, beef stew, freedom, poetry, Michelangelo, Mozart.

Why is it important to ground the word 'love'? Because 'love' is an undefined imaginary word and therefore we can assign it to a huge number of things, exactly because of its undefined nature. Undefined and inaccurate words in turn will produce undefined and inaccurate thoughts, and these inaccurate thoughts will result in inaccurate acts. And inaccurate is only the better end of a continuum the worse end of which includes trampling on the lives of millions of people or seizing world power.

Well, what is love then? It is high time to put things in

order. Love is nothing but a strategic feeling which, in terms of its function, serves the survival and well-being of another living creature. This definition assigns the series of feelings of sound 'love' to a group of feelings originating in internal interactions that I defined in my book *Feelings* and to the connections between the pieces of this group. I intend to skip the discussion of the details of this definition now because neither the topic nor the length of this book renders such discussion possible. If you are really interested, do not hesitate to consult my book *Feelings*.

What is the consequence of the definition above? That, with the help of an appropriate scientific apparatus, we can localise the areas or the cells in our brains that participate in the creation of the feeling of love and, in case of need, these cells can be further analysed at the level of biochemistry, chemistry and physics. In other words, we have grounded the word 'love' and connected it to the world through our own body: we have anchored it. So the series of feelings of sound 'love' in our mind is not an imaginary word anymore, instead it represents a real piece of the world because we have assigned the series of feelings of sound 'love' to processes taking place in our body and in this way we have linked it to the entire world as we are also part of the world. It has become immediately clear that of the list "I can love Julie, my parents, my children, my neighbour, my dog, my cat, beef stew, freedom, poetry, Michelangelo, Mozart", actually I can only love Julie, my parents, my children, my neighbour, my dog and my cat. With regard to the rest of the list, I have entirely different feelings. They may be equally nice feelings, but they are not the feeling of love but other orienting and marker feelings.

What did we just do? Why is it important? What is the significance of having grounded the tiny word 'love'? What significance can this whole hocus-pocus possibly have? Enormous significance! We have just turned thousands of tons of books sloppily raving about love into curios of science history and of literary history. And we did nothing other than interpret and ground one 'harmless' little word. Just consider how many less 'harmless' words may exist, the grounding of which could radically change the fate of the whole of humanity! With the grounding of each and every one of those words sciences and pseudo-sciences will disappear and millions of human lives will change fundamentally. Yes. This is not a game anymore. This is what the future of humankind may depend on!

11.

THE DATA NETWORK

Relations between words in people's heads try to map and reflect the relations and interactions taking place in the world, with more or less success. As a consequence, just as arbitrary units cannot form connections with each other in the real world, words, or series of feelings of sound, symbolising different parts of the world cannot form connections in people at will. See Figure 14.

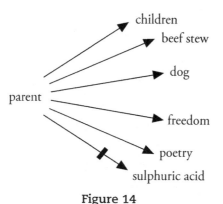

Figure 14

Figure 14 shows that we can connect the word parent to the words children, beef stew, dog, freedom and poetry but we cannot connect it to the word sulphuric acid, at least not directly. Words in our heads form a network of data in which it is defined which words you can connect to which other words. When we think with words, all we do is walk along this network of data from one word to another whilst observing the rules. That is, we can only jump from one word to another if it is allowed or, in other words, if there is a connection between the two words just as there is a connection between the two things in the real world we are mapping. Naturally, no one can prevent us connecting the word 'parent' with the word 'sulphuric acid' but this connection will have nothing to do with the mapping of the world in exactly the same way as when we connect the words love and beef stew to one another.

Before defining the word love, we could have connected the word love to each and every word of Figure 14, except the word sulphuric acid. See Figure 15

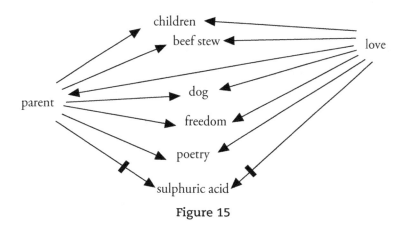

Figure 15

After defining and anchoring the word love, we now have the situation shown in Figure 16.

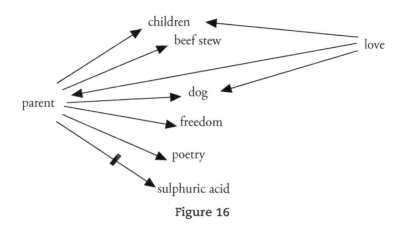

Figure 16

So we cannot connect the word love to the words beef stew, freedom and poetry any more. The result is that each and every theory created and each and every piece of writing written in the past about loving beef stew, freedom and poetry loses its meaning, and it becomes impossible to create such connections in the future.

Do we need to ground all imaginary words? No, we do not, for God's sake! There is a large group of imaginary words that it is not always useful to ground. Which is this group? The words used by the science of mathematics. Numbers are series of feelings of sound that represent imaginary words because there is no one, two or three in the world around us. I mean, I have never seen any 'one' or 'two' neither in the street, nor on the bus, nor on the tram. Not to mention the fact that only one instance of anything exists in the world around us and it is impossible to have two or three of something because there are no two things that are identical in the world. Consequently, when we are using the means of mathematics, like it or not, we change dimensions and move automatically to the imaginary world.

When I was a high school student, I read a very interesting book. The title was *Summa Technologiae*. The book was written by Stanislaw Lem, one of the greatest science fiction writers of the 20th century. There was a very interesting and relevant thought in this book. Lem compared the mathematician to a tailor who makes all the items of clothes that can be imagined, ignoring the real world in the meantime. He does not care if these clothes will suit anyone or if they can be used for anything. He carries out his work according to accurately defined principles and the only thing he cares about is that his principles do not contradict each other. At the back of the tailor's workshop, there is a storage room where he stores completed clothes. There are clothes for people and clothes for plants in his storage room, there are some that suit a submarine but there are also some that do not suit anybody or anything. From time to time people come to the tailor and search through the clothes. They are holding something in one hand and try to put the clothes on it with the other hand. Sometimes it works, sometimes it does not. What is the lesson of this story? The connections of the words used in mathematics are defined by strict rules. See Figure 17.

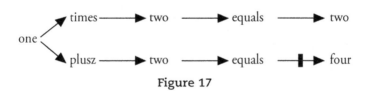

Figure 17

Just as in the case of simple words, we cannot connect just any word with any other word in mathematics either. But while in the case of simple words, the connectability of the words is defined by how accurately the resulting connection describes the world, in the case of mathematics, the main principle is observing the predefined rules. Mathematics does not care about mapping or describing the world, all it cares about is its own principles. That is why it makes nice little clothes that do not suit anyone.

The world of numbers is a perfectly sterile imaginary world. Do we need it? Absolutely. (You can always find useful things in a vintage clothes shop.) Do we need to ground the world of numbers? We can, if there is need to. How can we ground the world of numbers? The easiest thing is to assign such notions to numbers that have many connections and links to the world around us. For example, 1 apple + 2 apples = 3 apples, 1 nuclear reactor + 2 nuclear reactors = 3 nuclear reactors. And this is the good thing about it! Numbers are universal. I can assign them to various things. The moment of assigning numbers to something is exactly the same moment as when somebody manages to find some clothes in the tailor's store and puts them on something.

Of course, you cannot ground every mathematic formula. You can make sense of the equation 1 person + 2 persons = 3 persons, but you cannot interpret . You can, however, interpret the formula 1 person / 2. That one is called murder and it is considered a crime. The degree of groundedness of numbers depends on how much the words assigned to them are grounded. 1 minus child + 2 minus children = 3 minus children. Of course, you cannot talk about grounding in this case.

To summarise what has been said in this chapter, which words in the network of data people can connect with which other words is defined either by strict rules – see mathematics – or by the processes and interactions taking place in the external world. Or so you may think. But that is not the case at all.

12.

THE RELATION BETWEEN WORDS AS SERIES OF FEELINGS OF SOUND AND OTHER FEELINGS

After dealing so much with grounding words that any electrician would be happy to employ us as apprentices, let us go on with our research. Is it only possible to connect a word, a series of feelings of sound, to another word? Or can we connect other feelings to words? The answer to this question is clear and it comes from the definition of word itself. In the case of non-imaginary words, many different kinds of feelings can be connected to a given series of feelings of sound, i.e. word. When we heard the series of feelings of sound 'apple' for the first time, no other feelings were connected to it. But while we were eating an apple for the first time, a number of different feelings appeared in us and not only were these feelings present while we were eating the apple but they also became connected to the series of feelings of sound 'apple' in a way that we can recall them later on. See Figure 18.

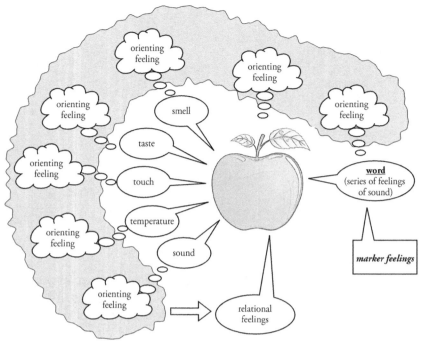

Figure 18

Recalling the apple in our mind, we will find that the feelings shown in the figure are not saved in our memory with the same intensity. This is perfectly natural. In order to prevent overloading our memory, we only save the most important feelings. The feeling that is the most important for us will act as the base feeling. In the case of the apple, the base feeling was the image of the apple itself or, to be more accurate, the pattern of nervous excitement generated in us while we were looking at the apple. It is called the base feeling because this is the 'image' to which other 'incoming' feelings – the feelings of smell, touch, temperature and sound – are connected. In this case, the word 'feelings of sound' only refers to sounds experienced while eating the apple, although it can also refer to the sound of an apple falling off the tree or any other sounds originating from an interaction between the apple and its environment (apples usually do not hum tunes softly when they alone).

You can see that further orienting feelings are connected to our 'incoming' feelings, and these show us if we find a given feeling pleasant, neutral or unpleasant in the given moment. There is another feeling above the image of the apple itself that shows whether we find the image of the apple beautiful or ugly. As a matter of fact, orienting feelings belong to 'relational feelings', the only reason they were given a separate category was to lead to better understanding. In the bottom of the figure, you can see the bubble 'relational feelings'. These feelings are guiding signs that define how we should relate to a given phenomenon and what we should do, and how we should do it, in relation to that phenomenon. Relational feelings include need-indicating feelings – for example, hunger – orienting feelings, strategic feelings – for example desire, disgust, joy, mental pain, anger or love – and tactical feelings. Some of these feelings are based on experience gained in the past and some of them reflect the current state of affairs.

On the right-hand-side of Figure 18, the word 'word' appears, which is nothing else but a series of feelings of sound. It may be worth mentioning that there is an orienting feeling connected to the word 'word' also which tells us if that particular word triggers pleasant or unpleasant feelings in us. And in the bottom right of Figure 18, you can see 'marker feelings'. As we will see later on, this is a very special type of feeling which is very important in terms of speaking and thinking.

Although the various feelings in this example are assigned to the nervous excitement obtained through seeing the apple or, to be more simple, assigned to the image of the apple, so we can recall the feelings shown in Figure 18 in connection with the image, these connections actually also work the other way round. In other words, the smell, the taste or the touch of the apple can also remind us of the image of the apple. Still it is beyond dispute that the rest of the feelings are primarily connected to the image of the apple. The image of the apple activates all the other feelings shown in Figure 18. That means in this particular a case, our base feeling is the pattern of nervous excitement generated in us while looking at the apple.

Another important thing to note is that the feelings shown in the left-hand side of Figure 18 were formed earlier than the ones connected to speech shown in the right-hand side both in our ontogeny and phylogeny. And not only were they formed earlier, they are able to exist independently, whereas the ones on the right-hand side cannot exist alone: the feelings on the left-hand side give basis to their existence.

Naturally these feelings can be different for different objects. For example, in the case a piece of stone, the feelings of taste or smell will definitely be missing. In the case of other words, we will also see different kinds of base feelings. Let us take a nice smell for example, driven towards us by the wind. Let us have a look at Figure 19.

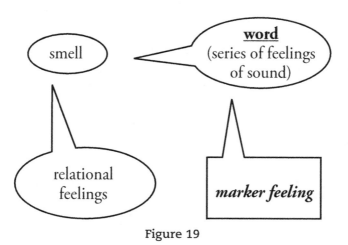

Figure 19

Due to the nature of things, we can see that the number of feelings has been reduced in Figure 19 as compared to Figure 18. In Figure 19, the base feeling is clearly smell. We can draw a similar chart for an unknown tune or an unknown taste. In these cases, the base feeling would always be the feeling we are examining. And what is the situation in the world of imaginary words? Let us have a look at Figure 20.

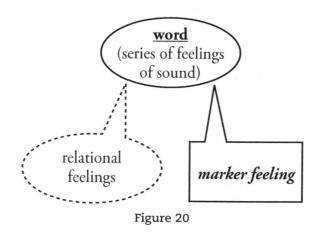

Figure 20

Sterile imaginary words do not have roots in reality or, to be more precise, they do not have reference points or feelings in the world around us. What happens in such a case? The most important thing that we notice is that the series of feelings of sound constituting the word becomes the base feeling itself. That is the rest of the feelings are connected to the series of feelings of sound constituting the word. You must have noticed the bubble of the dotted line around 're- lational feelings'. I use the dotted line because these feel- ings, even if not completely lost, have been reduced in num- ber or transformed in part as we will see later. The question might arise whether it is possible at all to further reduce the number of feelings connected to a word. Can we think of a word no other feelings are directly connected to? The answer is yes or, more precisely, almost yes. In these cases, it makes no sense to talk about a base feeling because only the word itself is present and no other feelings are connect- ed to it. These words are free of any other additional feelings and they are nothing else but the series of feelings of sound symbolising numbers: one, two, three…

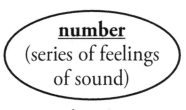

number
(series of feelings
of sound)

Figure 21

Although theoretically there are some orienting feelings formed in us in connection with the sound of numbers, their effect is negligible so we can simply disregard them. There may be other relational feelings present sometimes which are also not shown in Figure 21 because they are not connected to every number but only to a couple of them and, even then, only incidentally, depending on the given person. These are the feelings based on superstition that are connected to certain numbers (for example number 13) in certain people. Or there are feelings that can be connected to pleasant or unpleasant experiences of our past. In most cases however, we see that the series of feelings of sound representing numbers are practically 'sterile', no other feelings are connected to them. And this fact has enormous importance!

The fact that engineers can design aeroplanes is partly down to the fact that, apart from using high accuracy words, engineers also use words to which practically no other feelings are connected: one, two, three… Why is it important? Because the feelings connected to certain words will influence the direction and efficiency of our thinking and can divert our thoughts in ways we do not even notice. Let us look at an example. Let us take a simple equation: $3 - 1 = 2$. It is nice and clear for everyone. As long as we are in the imaginary world of mathematics, it works properly. Although, at the moment when we try to use our mathematical knowledge in practice – that is at the moment we ground numbers – the feelings connected to numbers appear right away or, to be more precise, the feelings carried by the words used for grounding numbers are spread to numbers as well. For example: three apples – 1 apple = two apples. Let us solve this equation. We can only deduct one apple from three apples if we eat one apple because if we only put it aside, the apple will still exist so our statement would not hold water. We can only realise the content of our equation if we eat one apple. Let us now have a similar equation with cuddly little white bunnies. 3 bunnies – 1 bunny = 2 bunnies. In order to solve the equation, let us cut the throat of one of our bunnies. While blood is spattering everywhere and our little bunny is squirming with its eyes dimming, we can consider whether we make a soup or a stew out of it. I suppose different feelings are whirling in you now than when we were solving the equation $3 - 1 = 2$ only with numbers in the imaginary world of mathematics. The dark times of humankind also confirm that numbers are sterile and free of feelings. People did not have names in the death camp of Auschwitz. A number was tattooed on everyone so the executors had an easier job. Their conscience – if we can talk about such a thing in their case – digested operations carried out with numbers more easily.

13.

THE EFFECT OF FEELINGS ON THINKING

I must apologise for the inaccurate title but I chose this one because it is more easily understandable for people who have just started to familiarise themselves with the world of feelings. As a matter of fact, the title *The interactions of feelings during the mapping of our world* would have been more accurate, since when feelings of the traditional sense influence our thinking, all they do is interact with other types of feelings including series of feelings of sound, i.e. words. The most obvious example that everyone has experienced is when our feelings of the traditional sense influence our speech, or in other words, our thinking aloud. In these cases, which any inexperienced observer can notice, our tone and intonation changes, our voice may tremble and choke, we may start stammering and so on. But I would like to take you on a different trip, my dear reader. I suggest that we try to shed light on the processes that define the direction of our thinking. In order to better understand the process of the interaction between feelings, let us look at the role feelings play in our lives.

13.1 The controlling role of feelings in our lives

My dear reader, together you and I have found out that in our internal world – the only world that exists for us – only feelings exist. Consequently, only feelings can control our lives because there is nothing else in our internal world. You may rightly ask on what basis do our feelings control our lives, and in what directions do they try to lead us. During the millions of years of phylogeny, a complex and hierarchic control system of feelings developed in various species. We humans are no exceptions. This control system, as all good control systems do, follows an order of priority the primary goal of which is existence itself, and the maintenance of this existence at the level of both the individual and the species. In the case of humanity, this control system is much more sophisticated than in the case of animals. It uses all the capacities and capabilities of humans but the final goal of it is also to ensure our existence.

The goals that appear in the process of control, and their priorities and relations to one another, can best be shown in a hierarchy of needs in which those needs, built on top of one another, form a strongly connected system as shown below:

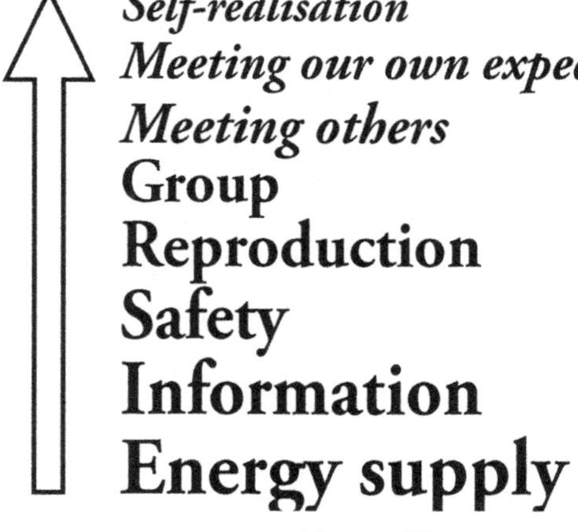

Self-realisation
Meeting our own expectations
Meeting others
Group
Reproduction
Safety
Information
Energy supply

Figure 22

As you can see, I indicated the top three levels of the needs hierarchy in italics. I did so in order to point out that these needs only appear in us, humans, and they cannot be found in animals since you need speech for the formation of these needs at the top levels of our hierarchy. The needs at the lower five levels: energy supply, information, safety, reproduction and group needs, however, can be found in more developed animals. At the lower five levels, control is carried out by feelings of the traditional sense including need-indicating, orienting, strategic, technological and status indicating feelings. Therefore, these needs belong to the level of traditional feeling-based control, whereas the needs of the top three levels belong to the level of symbol-based control that uses words.

This way, we have managed to break up the control of human behaviour into two apparently independent levels. This approach, however, only serves the purpose of better understanding. As a matter of fact, these levels control our activities and fate in close cooperation with, and not at all independent from, each other. And we must not overlook the fact that the level we called the level of symbol-based control is nothing else but the level of control based on series of feelings of sound. This is also a level of feeling-based control, only in this case it is not feelings of the traditional sense but a special type of feelings: feelings of sound. Consequently, when ladies with tears in their eyes and sighs on their lips ask the question: "Shall I listen to my heart (feelings) or my head?", they will listen to their feelings either way.

Naturally, feelings do not only control our activities but also our thinking. This fact is far from being obvious for most of us. But part of our feelings provides motivation for thinking, without which motivation our thoughts could not even be formed. Another part of our feelings, on the other hand, controls the direction of trains of thoughts that have already been started.

The simplest example of motivation is need-indicating feelings such as hunger, thirst, tiredness, fear or loneliness. But of course, other feelings may also encourage us to think, for example, orienting feelings and strategic feeling such as desire, disgust, joy, mental pain and anger, as well as status indicating feelings. Consequently, the two levels form an indivisible unit. Let us start our investigation with the level of traditional feeling-based control. At this level, our activities are aimed at avoiding unpleasant feelings and experiencing as many pleasant feelings as possible. (See Figure 23)

Figure 23

In Figure 23, I have indicated unpleasant feelings to be avoided with black spots and pleasant feelings to be enjoyed with white spots.

Feeling-based and symbol-based controls, however, are there in us at the same time, and they work in a parallel fashion to realise their goals. For example, if the feeling of hunger appears, the symbol-based control immediately joins in in order to fill our stomach and to avoid the unpleasant feeling of hunger. That is, we start thinking:

"Oh, my God, I'm really hungry. I should get some food. Now, where do I find something to eat?" In order to make it easier to understand, I show the levels of feeling-based and symbol-based controls in the same image. (See Figure 24)

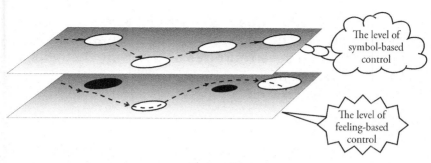

The level of symbol-based control

The level of feeling-based control

Figure 24

In Figure 24, the black spot on the left of the level of feeling-based control represents the unpleasant and avoidable feeling of hunger, whereas the white spot on the left of the level of feeling-based control represents the pleasant orienting feelings experienced while eating food. The other black spot on the right of the level of feeling-based control represents the unpleasant feeling of thirst after eating, whereas the other white spot represents the pleasant orienting feelings experienced during drinking.

You can see that the thoughts on the symbol-based control level are more or less in synchrony with the events taking place on the feeling-based control level. If an unpleasant and avoidable feeling appears on the feeling-based control level, the processes appearing on the symbol-based control level try to avoid it in cooperation with the feeling-based level. Of course, it may also happen that the symbol-based control runs ahead, so to speak, and tries to avoid an unpleasant feeling even before it appears.

It is a bit of a detour but it is worth mentioning that while on the feeling-based control level feelings follow the course of events in a continuous transition, on the level of symbol-based control, events are followed by jumping from discrete symbol to discrete symbol as there are no interpretable fields or transitions between words.

Levels of control may also switch into an independent

mode of operation, for example during skiing. While I am automatically moving around dangerous humps and trying to find smooth and even surfaces of snow, my thoughts are running far away and I may be thinking about the evening programme. (See Figure 25)

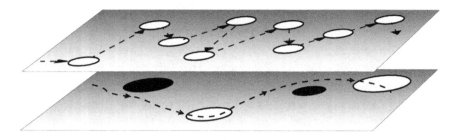

Figure 25

People use a combination of three different methods for thinking and for solving problems. Depending on the type of the problem, these ways of thinking can be used independently or together in close cooperation. We will now briefly outline these methods in order to also examine how our feelings of the traditional sense influence and guide our thoughts.

13.2 Eureka

This is the first, and probably the oldest, method of thinking. It does not follow the principles of logic so it is not a traditional form of thinking. You might call it recognition, a sudden realisation or a snap and therefore, it is a one-off, non-reproducible process. This is a situation everyone knows so well, when you simply wake up to the solution in a moment. Most of the time, you cannot even formulate your thoughts immediately after that particular moment, you are only certain that you have found the solution. Then you start making efforts to put the solution into a logical verbal form. This process works pretty much like a jigsaw puzzle when some pieces are still missing from the picture we have already put together and then we suddenly realise where the pieces in our hands will fit. Sometimes this kind of realisation, or enlightenment, does not take place in a moment but requires a longer time. In such cases we already 'know' or, to be more accurate, suspect where the given piece of the jigsaw puzzle should go but it somehow does not fit the whole picture. This is when we start turning the given piece around and try to fit it in. In such a case, the process is controlled and closed by feelings of shorter or longer duration appearing on the feeling-based control level. The process is usually started by some of our need-indicating feelings, then an orienting feeling joins in, while the strategic feeling of desire urges us to carry on accompanied by the technological feeling of tension in case of an obstacle, and the process is closed by the strategic feeling of joy and the technological feeling of laxity. At least this is the 'Eureka' scenario.

But the 'Eureka' scenario is not the only one. There is also an 'anti-Eureka' scenario but that is much more difficult to grasp. While we are trying to fit our little piece of puzzle into the picture, we already have an idea, even if we cannot put it in words, of what kind of picture we are going to have. And this is a very important moment! Let us call this point the point of foreboding. This is where it becomes clear whether we will follow the 'Eureka' or the 'anti-Eureka' scenario as we can follow two paths from this point on. If it is a positive picture that is unfolding for us, we will pursue it because of the feelings of desire and tension and we will urge ourselves to try and fit the missing piece into the big picture and finally, at some later time, we will put the solution into words. But if the picture that is evolving from our presentiments triggers some unpleasant feelings in us, these feelings put an end to the entire process in the blink of an eye. We do not push the process to the end, we do not let the missing piece fit in the big picture we do not like. We beat a retreat from the unpleasant recognition. This is the 'anti-Eureka' scenario. How can I make these processes more graphic? Look at Figure 26.

Figure 26

The spontaneous process is symbolised by a ball rolling away and swimming randomly at the level of feeling-based control and which suddenly finds the solution. The use of the word 'random', is purely figurative. There are no random feelings. More accurate wording would be that we find the solution through experiencing feelings not aimed at finding the given solution, feelings that are indifferent in the given case. The 'Eureka' scenario is shown in Figure 27.

Figure 27

In Figure 27, the movement of the ball is ensured by the fact that we raise the plane a little on the side opposite to the white spot representing the solution, and the ball, under the impact of gravity, starts rolling towards the solution. In this picture, the field of gravity symbolises the indispensable elements of the 'Eureka' scenario, the feelings that urge us to reach the given goal. Just as gravity navigates the ball to the white spot, our feelings navigate us into the direction of finding a solution to a problem. This is not a 'random' process any more, instead it is a targeted effort which, in case of success, is crowned with the feeling of joy. Archimedes also shouted out because he felt joy.

Let us see what the situation is with the 'anti-Eureka' scenario. This scenario is shown in Figure 28.

Figure 28

In Figure 28, we use gravity again but not in order to find the goal or the solution but, on the contrary, to avoid it. In the 'anti-Eureka' scenario, a decisive role is given to feelings which imperceptibly divert us from the solution. Many feelings can participate in both the 'Eureka' and the 'anti-Eureka' scenarios. All these feelings are dependent on the given individual and the given situation but I am not going to give a detailed outline of them since this is not the subject of my book. To sum up what we have said so far, feelings connected to the phenomena of the world previously generated or imprinted in us determine this method of our thinking in a way that remains almost unnoticed for us and it takes much concentration, self-awareness and experience to find their trace.

13.3 The comic strip

The second method of thinking or problem-solving uses images. I can say to myself, for example, that "I'll go down to the shop." But I can also replace this train of thought with imagining how I step out of the front door of my flat, how I walk down the street to the shop, how I open the door and enter. This way of thinking is more widespread among people who can use the advantages of this method in their jobs, for example, architects, engineers, internal designers or all kinds of artists, painters and sculptors. These people have to think through and plan in advance how the different pieces will be positioned in relation to one another in the space and what effect they will cause.

It is much easier to notice and understand the effect of feelings of the traditional sense in this sort of thinking. We simply like imagining scenes that are attractive for us and we detest evoking images that are fearful, disgusting or heart-breaking for us. These processes are shown in Figures 27 and 28. It is worth pointing out that orienting feelings have an important, if not exclusive, role in these cases.

You can see that our feelings have a strong influence on this way of thinking as well. For example, if someone was raised to think that sex was a disgusting and sinful thing coming from Satan himself, that person would probably try to avoid visualising huge orgies (or perhaps they would only say so☺). And those who have a different opinion on sex... But to use a more innocent example, an architect who likes the modern style will hardly ever visualise antique shapes while preparing her designs because she connects pleasant orienting feelings to modern lines and not antique shapes. The disadvantage of this method of thinking is that it operates with too large databases and so it is sometimes slow and difficult to use. And, on the other hand, we cannot use this method to think about sounds, smells, tastes or tactile feelings – all other types of feelings except visual ones, for that matter – because these things do not have 'images' so we cannot visualise them.

13.4 The river of words

Where does the river flow? The third, and most tradition-al, way of thinking is based on manipulation with words, or symbols. As the dear reader must have guessed, though, the process does not take place exclusively at the level of sym-bol-based control: the level of feeling-based control is also involved. If I wanted to put it simply, the bottom line is that we are trying to avoid any kind of thoughts the result – or 'projection' appearing at the level of feeling-based control – of which triggers unpleasant feelings in us and we like play-ing with thoughts the result – or 'projection' appearing at the level of feeling-based control – of which triggers pleas-ant feelings in us.

In order to make things easier to understand, let us start with the results. We like thinking, or sometimes day-dreaming, about goals the reaching of which results in experiencing pleasant feelings. We like thinking about, for example, organising our wedding. These processes are best demonstrated in Figure 27. The more we are attract-ed to someone, the more we cherish the thought and the harder it is to divert our thoughts from the goal. A good example is the phenomenon older generations probably know very well called the 'deaf bride, deaf bridegroom syndrome' (younger generations will have ample time and opportunity to experience this phenomenon later). The essence of the phenomenon is that it is as plain as it gets for the parents, for the grandparents, for the friends, for the neighbours and practically for the entire galaxy that nothing good will come out of the marriage in question. But no matter if hundreds of 1000 watt speakers roar into the ears of the bride and the bridegroom: "DON'T DO IT! DON'T BE A FOOL!" it is completely hopeless to warn the victims. The process shown in Figure 27 cannot be stopped and cannot be influenced either. Anyone who tries it will be a nasty and evil person in the eyes of the victims. The desire trap in these cases is so deep that the victims are simply incapable of thinking any negative thoughts that would put the future marriage at risk.

The direct opposite of this is the 'parent's prayer' phenomenon when parents beg their child to learn. This scenario is demonstrated in Figure 28. The child does not feel like learning at all so he tries to avoid any thoughts related to the toil of learning and to the eerie consequences of not learning. He simply does not think about poverty and need, his thoughts follow the procedure shown in Figure 27 instead, he only thinks about what a nice party he will have tonight with his friends.

As for the effects the projections of our thoughts at the level of feeling-based control have on our thinking, things are much trickier here. Processes are much more difficult to catch. In order to better understand the phenomenon, let us examine a handful of examples. Let us start with a joke. A guy is travelling on a train together with a very good-looking woman:

'Excuse me, my lady, would you sleep with me for one million dollars?' The woman thinks for a short while and says:

'Yes, why not?'

'And would you sleep with me for ten dollars?'

'You arrogant stinker! Who do think I am?'

'I'm sorry, my lady, but we have already found out who you are. We're only negotiating the price now.'

Many women who sleep with men for money think they only do it because of temporary financial hardships and they are not whores. Not to mention marriages of propriety where the bride goes to bed with a rich guy in exchange for a huge settlement. That is, she screws for money so she is a whore. As in the definition of the word 'whore' it is not quantified how many people you need to offer your services to or how much money should be at stake. Of course, it is not very likely that any fortune-hunting woman would call herself a whore. In their thoughts or in their speech they avoid using the word 'whore' in relation to their own person because that would cause mental pain for them.

As another example, someone I know offered to give me a lift the other day. While we were travelling, he tried to change lanes without looking in the rear view mirror and as a result, we almost had a crash. 'Where did you get your driving licence? You idiot!' he was shouting. And then after a little while he added: 'It is these speeding dummies that cause all the accidents.' Needless to say that the driver of the other car was driving in a perfectly orderly way. My acquaintance, however, was trying to blame the other driver for the whole mishap, while he did not even consider the thought that he himself may have made a mistake. He did not even consider the thought because if he had, he would have had to attach words such as inattentive or clumsy – or as he said 'idiot' and 'dummy' – to himself. But connecting these words to himself trigger rather unpleasant feelings at the level of feeling-based control.

There are much more sorrowful stories as well. There was an old lady living in a village who had saved a little money from all the hard work in her life in order to go to an old people's home where she would get proper service when she became really old. As time passed, it became more and more difficult to do the housework, she had pains here and there and she got really tired. Finally she felt that it was time to go to the old people's home to spend the rest of her life in a more or less dignified way. But then the grandson of the lady, a 'genius' of an entrepreneur, appeared and borrowed the money the lady had saved and even took out a mortgage on her house. Needless to say, the money and the house, the fruits of the toil of a lifetime, went down the drain. And what was the first reaction of the glorious entrepreneur? 'What the heck does she need all that money for? She has managed to survive this far so she will survive now. She does not have so much time anyway.' He did not even consider the thought 'What an idiot I was that I abused the love of my grandmother and ruined the whole life of a person with my irresponsible and crazy ambition.' It is completely natural that these thoughts are not considered in his mind because they would really hurt. Probably he was raised to think that it was always somebody else's fault. It is very comfortable like that... It often happens that we happily acquire strange theories or thoughts in order to cover our own faults and in order to avoid facing our own mistakes. The commonest example is the 'fate theory'. The reason my life is what it is is not that I was lazy, that I did not learn and did not work, that I was a coward, that I made bad decisions but it was fate or God's will that arranged it so.

The common feature of the stories above is that the protagonists are trying to avoid each and every word or thought that would trigger unpleasant feelings in them if used in connection with themselves. But why? What is the mechanism that works in such cases? To answer these questions, we need to dig a little deeper.

13.4.1 Marker feelings

When thinking in 'images' we manipulate patterns of nervous excitement originating from interactions between us and the external world, however, when thinking in words, i.e. series of feelings of sound, the situation is entirely different. Words are only symbols. Words are not patterns of nervous excitement of interactions with the external world anymore, they are only symbols of them. Yes, I know, you need to hear each word at least once, but the series of feelings of sound 'sea' does not have much to do with the patterns of nervous excitement triggered by the sight, the murmur, the salty taste or the cool touch of the sea. When thinking in words, we carry out operations with symbols or series of feelings of sound and do not manipulate with patterns of nervous excitement generated in interactions with the external world.

Now, how do our feelings of the traditional sense affect our thinking in words? The answer is very simple: with the help of feelings attached to the words. I suggest going back to Figure 18. Looking at Figure 18, you may rightly exclaim: 'Good gracious, there are lots of feelings here!' And you are right. But... Let us take a simple example: 'I'll go down to the shop to buy some apples.' When we utter or hear this sentence, the feelings shown in Figure 18 become detached or wear off, so to speak, from the words of this sentence. I am not going to recall the visceral feelings appearing during my movements connected to the words 'go down'; neither will the image of the 'shop' appear in front of my mental eyes with its typical smell and sounds nor will I feel the coolness of the air conditioned facility; nor will the image, the smell, the taste and the touch of the apple wake in my mind. These feelings are not present while we are uttering, or listening to, this sentence. They simply become detached from the words of the sentence. And it is perfectly understandable and normal! Our mind has a finite capacity and it is impossible to recall all these feelings in such a short time. Or if we did recall them, we would die of hunger before reaching that apple.

So our brain, in order to achieve a more efficient operation, gets rid of all the unnecessary frills and concentrates on the essence. The many feelings shown in Figure 18 all disappear. Or rather, almost all. One group of them will definitely stay and this group is none other than the group of marker feelings. My dear reader may rightly ask what is the case then with literary works? When you are reading a good novel, letters almost come alive and we ourselves share the life of the protagonist to some extent: we see what she sees and feel what she feels. When we are reading a good description of a landscape, it is almost as if we were there. Feelings do not become detached from words at all, instead, words seem to carry all those feelings. It is so. But we are talking about different things at the same time.

The first and foremost thing to consider is the speed of thinking. Our thoughts sometimes break into a run and then stop a little to have a rest. When they are running, other feelings break off from the words and only marker feelings exert their effect, but when our thoughts have a rest, they follow one another at a slower pace and the other feelings connected to the word have time to unfold. Let us take this sentence as an example: 'At the weekend, we'll go down to the seaside to have some fun.' While I am uttering this sentence, only marker feelings connect to the word 'seaside' but if I stop for a short time after saying this sentence, the image of the seaside appears right away and I can almost feel the heat of the sun, the pleasant touch of the breeze and I can hear the noise of the people who are sunbathing on the beach.

The second thing to consider is the fact that completely different mental processes take place while we are constructing a sentence than while we are 'passively' reading. Constructing a sentence is always more complicated than reading. During the construction of a sentence, our brain carries out more complex operations that require higher levels of performance and therefore our brain is busier than when we are sitting in an armchair in front of the fire reading. When we are reading we have time to stop and have a rest or even to muse. We can give time to our brain to unfold and display all the feelings related to the words that we read, as we have shown in Figure 18.

And the third thing to consider is that writers do not usually compose their sentences in split seconds. They have time, so to speak, to digest, think over and polish their text and select the most appropriate, most powerful words to describe a situation. Moreover, they also use synonyms to reinforce the effect. All the above facts, however, do not change the importance of marker feelings at all. What is more, since literary works, by definition, are full of words, they are also full of marker feelings. And those marker feelings play their tricks.

Why did I give the name 'marker feelings' to these feelings? Because they connect to words as invisible, almost imperceptible little marks or flags. These marker feelings define which word we are using and which word we are avoiding in a given moment, that is, they influence the direction of our thinking. Let us look at an example. There is the joke in which, after a pleasant evening spent together, the guy asks his new lady love shyly:

'May I see you home?'

'Only if you wear a condom.'

What is the pun of the joke? The girl actually answers the unasked question 'Can I fuck you?' which is a rather obscene and bawdy expression. Attention! This is a very graphic and easy to understand example of marker feelings. Those of you who are more sensitive can now easily carry out a small experiment. Concentrate your attention on the feelings that arise in you while you are reading the word 'fuck'. In this situation, most of us experience a short and intensive feeling like a lash, which dies away slowly. The strength of the marker feelings that arise in such a situation changes from person to person because we each assign feelings of different intensity and direction to any given word. There are segments of society where this word functions as a conjunction and no one finds it problematic. Obscene and bawdy words, naturally, have been known to you before but if someone had asked you what these words were you probably would have answered only that these were 'rude or ugly' words. But you could not have explained why these words were 'rude or ugly' or what the notion of being beautiful or ugly has to do with the whole thing and what the word 'beauty' means, for that matter.

Oops! We have bumped into another, as yet ungrounded, imaginary word, the word 'beauty'. But I suggest that we don't digress at this point, but come back to the grounding of the word 'beauty' later.

As a matter of fact, we use quite a number of different

words or compounds to denote sexual intercourse and different marker feelings are attached to each one of them. While you are reading the list below, please pay particular attention to the marker feelings that arise in you and their continuous changes.

- fuck
- bang
- screw
- shag
- diddle
- have sex
- sleep with someone
- make love

Or let us read the following excerpt from a funeral oration: "We all feel desperate pain about your death, dear Joseph. Your children are overwhelmed to have to entomb their beloved father." Although the meaning of the words in the quotation above is exactly the same as in the one below, we still attach completely different marker feelings to them: "We all feel fucked that you kicked the bucket, Joe. Your kids also hate that they have to bury the daddy they dug so much." It is obvious from the examples above that our brain quickly selects the word that fits the situation from the pool of available words with similar meaning. We will always address our friend as the situation dictates and we will never mix the words of the two 'funeral operations'. How can we do that? With the help of marker feelings.

13.4.2 The formation of marker feelings

What are marker feelings? Marker feelings are nothing else but the essence of the relational feelings shown in Figure 18. While words, or series of feelings of sound, are symbols summarising incoming feelings shown in the left-hand side of Figure 18, marker feelings are summarised versions of the relational feelings shown in the left-hand side of Figure 18.

It is interesting to note that while we summarise incoming feelings by the use of series of feelings of sound, we do not summarise relational feelings as series of feelings of sound but we use essences of feelings instead. What is the reason? As a matter of fact, we do summarise a part of the relational feelings serving as the basis for marker feelings in the form of series of feelings of sound. When I say 'I fear' it symbolises the status indicating feeling of the need for security: fear, the words 'good', 'bad', 'beautiful', 'ugly' and 'fine' symbolise orienting feelings, the words 'attractive' and 'disgusting' symbolise strategic feelings and the words 'comfortable', 'hurried', 'hard' and 'patient' symbolise tactical feelings. Our thinking would look strange and would be slow and fragmented if we used words, or series of feelings of sound to denote relational feelings instead of marker feelings: "I'll buy (in a hurry) and apple (fine) in a shop (beautiful) and eat it (comfortably)." We must admit that it wouldn't work that way.

Marker feelings make it possible to quickly select the words that suit any given situation. In the case of imaginary words, if we look at Figure 20, we can see that 'relational feelings' are indicated with a dotted line. The reason is that these feelings are either hardly present or not present at all. As a consequence, it is almost exclusively marker feelings that influence or control our thinking with sterile imaginary words. Sadly, our thinking with sterile imaginary words becomes even more inaccurate and even more isolated from the world around us as a result.

How are marker feelings formed? Let's take two simple examples. We get on our favourite ski-plane and land in the vast ice fields of Greenland next to the igloo of an Eskimo. We put something into the hand of the Eskimo, who was brought out of his igloo by the noise of our engine, and since we do not speak a word in Eskimo, we try to convince the guy to eat the thing we gave him with vivid gestures. He has a careful look at it and sees that he is holding a red round

175

object of pleasant touch with a diameter of approximately 5 cm in his hand. He smells it and detects a nice smell. While he is taking a bite, he hears a crunchy sound, and a nice taste spreads in his mouth. While the Eskimo is chewing joyfully, we point at the object in his hand and repeat the word 'apple' several times with a meaningful expression on our face (it is not worth doing it too many times, because after a while he will think we are lunatics). Now we get back into the aeroplane and fly away. We come back the next day and explain to him with the help of an interpreter that the apple contains lots of vitamins and since it is rich in fibres, it helps digestion, and it has a beneficial effect on health.

What processes take place in the Eskimo's mind on the first day and on the second day? On the first day, while he is eating the apple, feelings coming from his interaction with the fruit get connected to the series of feelings of sound representing the word apple. Later the same day, he will remember how nice the apple tasted and smelled, how beautifully red its colour was and how crunchy it sounded under his teeth. During all this time, a marker feeling connected to the word apple is being formed on the basis of the relational feelings experienced during the interaction with the apple. The second day, when we tell him that the apple contains lots of vitamins, helps digestion and has beneficial effects on health, all we do is connect the marker feelings connected to the words 'vitamin' and 'health' to the marker feelings formed in him the previous day in connection with the word 'apple'. Marker feelings connected to the word 'apple', and formed as a result of the interactions with the apple, are broadened and modified with the marker feelings connected to the words 'vitamin' and 'health'.

The second example is when we play the procedure the other way round. We get out of the aeroplane with nothing in our hand, accompanied by an interpreter, and tell the guy that we will give him something we call 'apple' tomorrow and this thing is full of vitamins and is beneficial to health.

Then, the next day we give him the apple which he joyfully eats.

What's the difference between the two scenarios? A great deal. In the first case, the thinking of the Eskimo will be influenced by marker feelings generated during his interaction with the apple or, in other words, by feelings that are the result of his interactions with the external world. To put it in a more inaccurate but more easily understandable way, the external world serves as a base for his thinking. In the second case, his thinking will be influenced by marker feelings connected to the words 'vitamin' and 'health'. To put it in a more inaccurate but more easily understandable way, his marker feelings will not be based on the external world but on an imaginary world.

Why is it important? Because in the second case, the word 'apple', from the subjective point of view of our Eskimo, is only a notion or an imaginary word and his thinking with this word will be influenced by the marker feelings connected to the words 'vitamin' and 'health'. And very often this is exactly the case with the propagators of human studies. Their thinking is primarily controlled – and sometimes misguided – by marker feelings connected to imaginary words that do not have reference points in the external world.

Shall we make it a little more graphic and a little easier to understand? Let us get on our aeroplane again and, with the help of our interpreter, let us tell our friend that the next day he will be given a lethal instrument to which lots of blood has stuck throughout human history, and which has caused the death of millions. Needless to say, the poor guy will stress himself out the rest of the day about what kind of horrible thing we want to give him. And he does so only because his thinking is determined by the marker feelings connected to the words 'blood' and 'death'. After our poor friend has spent a sleepless night with his nightmares, the next day we give him a knife so he has something to peel the apple with.

'Oh, c'mon! This is all a load of rubbish.' you may think now. 'It is theoretically possible that marker feelings may have a little influence on the way philosophers locked up in their ivory towers think, but in practice, in everyday life, they have absolutely no significance. This is simply nonsense.' Are you sure? If we are already talking about death, murder and killing, let us examine how the very strongly negative marker feelings connected to these words influence the way people think.

The Ten Commandments of the Old Testament of the Bible, thousands of books and millions of newspaper articles tell us it is a sin to kill and to take others' lives. They treat the issue at great length, supported with all kinds of arguments and logical reasoning to prove why it is forbidden to kill. But most people do not even notice that killing is an organic part of our life and murderers are all around us. Why not? Because our thoughts are diverted by marker feelings. Humankind takes billions of lives every day: thousands of tonnes of fish are caught from the oceans, the necks of millions of poultry are cut and tens of thousands of pigs and cows are slaughtered every day. Naturally, you will immediately think: 'But one needs to eat! This is not real killing. This does not count.' Oops! This is exactly the moment when your thoughts are influenced by the marker feelings connected to killing! This is exactly the moment we were waiting for. It is here. Examine it carefully.

But let us move on. People do not only kill to get food but also because of boredom, in order to have fun or simply out of pleasure. Just think of fishing or hunting. 'Oh, come on. Wildlife needs regulating. If the populations proliferate, they will eat our crops.' I can almost hear the excuses. Do you really want to tell us that you only spend the freezing nights in the wilderness and pay serious sums of money to the hunting associations because you want to make a sacrifice to society? If society is so important for you, why don't you rather give the money to orphanages? No! The fact is that hunters actually enjoy killing but this is something you cannot admit either to yourself, or to others. It would be saying you are a murderer. Instead of the word 'murderer', you prefer using the word 'hunter'. Why? Because of marker feelings. Different marker feelings are attached to the word 'hunter' than to the word 'murderer'. Marker feelings divert our thoughts. People do not – or more accurately they cannot because of marker feelings – want to consider what they do and they do not want to be called murderers. Of course, somehow hunters also feel the inappropriateness of their thinking and they feel some sort of guilt. At least this is what the heavily decorated trophy displays after hunting suggest. They 'pay respect' to the wild animals they have killed. Would not it be simpler to 'pay respect' while they are still alive?

But let us move on again. Have you ever considered the fact that death, killing and murder provide the livelihood of millions of people? Yes, it is true. You can make a lot of money with death. Of course, only with effective death, not with handicraft, manual killing. The goal is to kill as many people as possible in the most efficient way. It requires accurate, sophisticated and scientific work. It is not just killing in a random fashion with low efficiency without scientific basis! Where do you think you are? This is exactly the goal the 'defence industry' serves. The name itself tells us everything. They do not call it the 'offence industry', manufacturing of manslaughter machinery or killing industry, they shyly use the term 'defence'. Why? Because positive marker feelings are connected to the word 'defence' in people's minds. It is all perfectly natural because never in the history of humankind have weapons been used for offence, only for defence. Funny, isn't it? But this is true, only it was not the defence of people but the defence of interests. Because people's lives do not matter much if somebody's interests require them.

And what is the situation with the training of murderers? Oh, come on. Don't pretend that you don't understand what

I am talking about. You know: the schools where people are taught how to kill. I am sure you know. The schools where they teach you how to stab someone in the stomach and how to spill someone's guts. You know, in an attack when there is a bayonet in the end of your rifle. Military schools. That is what I am talking about. Do you disagree? Do you think that rosy-minded young boys and girls are taught how to plant flowers in military schools? 'Okay, but how can you call protectors of the homeland murderers?' you may ask. Why shouldn't I? Because totally different marker feelings are attached to the word 'murderer' than to the word 'protector '. And our brain does everything to avoid unpleasant feelings when thinking. We start explaining things and come up with excuses like there is a need for soldiers and so on. The soldiers on the other side of the front line are the murderers, our soldiers are protectors even if our soldiers attacked the given country first. We have clever intelligence officers, our enemies have spies and dirty finks. The words intelligence officer, spy and fink mean exactly the same, only the marker feelings attached to them are different. Do you still say marker feelings do not influence our thinking?

13.4.3 The operation mechanism of marker feelings

Let us take the relationship between the words 'I' and 'clumsy' for example. Can we connect these two words easily? Well, speaking for myself, it triggers an unpleasant feeling in me if I need to connect these two words, although I can be really ham-fisted sometimes. Let us try to show it in a drawing. See Figure 29.

$$I \longrightarrow clumsy$$

Figure 29

Figure 29 represents how ancient philosophers imagined human thinking. They believed in the omnipotence, superiority and feeling-free nature of rationality and cold logic. For them, the space of human thinking is linear, uniform and free of distortion, a place where human trains of thought can pursue their goals in unswerving lines. But this is far from being true. Figure 29 is only one side of the coin or, more accurately, one level of thinking in words: the level of symbol-based control. But we should not forget about the level of feeling-based control either. Let us add the level of feeling-based control to Figure 29.

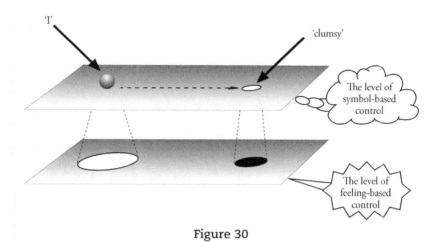

Figure 30

Figure 30 shows that actually this process takes place at two levels at the same time. The events taking place at the two levels, however, are not independent from one another. They are in interaction with each other as – do not forget – these are only symbolic levels. In reality, there are feelings at the level of symbol-based control as well, only they are a special type of feelings, namely series of feelings of sound. Figure 30 tries to demonstrate that words at the level of symbol-based control have projections, so to speak, at the level of feeling-based control. To put it more simply, feelings are connected to words. In the previous chapters, we have seen in detail what feelings are connected to different words and how. Since Figure 30 shows a dynamic train of thought and not a static one, most of the feelings connected to the words have become detached from them and only marker feelings are connected to the words. The large white spot at the level of feeling-based control represents the positive marker feelings connected to the word 'I', whereas the smaller black spot represents the negative marker feelings connected to the word 'clumsy'. What happens if we connect the two words? Let's look at Figure 31.

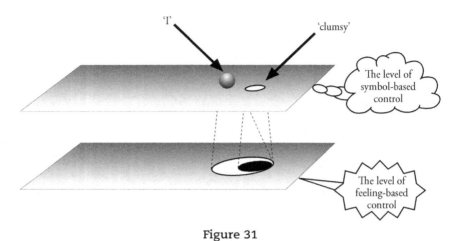

Figure 31

The black spot representing the negative marker feelings bites off, so to speak, a piece of the white spot representing positive marker feelings and therefore reduces the surface of the light spot significantly. It means that if I attach words with negative marker feelings to the word ‚I', that will reduce the positive marker feelings connected to the word 'I' which triggers the strategic feeling of mental pain. What is going to happen? Since we do not want to experience the feeling of mental pain, we try to avoid it somehow, as is shown in Figure 32.

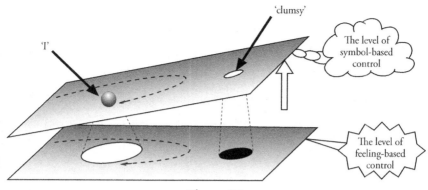

Figure 32

Due to the feeling of the expected mental pain, the level of the symbol-based control tilts a little so that the painful meeting does not come about. What happens if we replace the word 'clumsy' with the word 'clever'? That sounds much better. For me personally, it feels particularly nice if someone tells me I am clever. I feel proud. How might we picture that? Take a look at Figure 33.

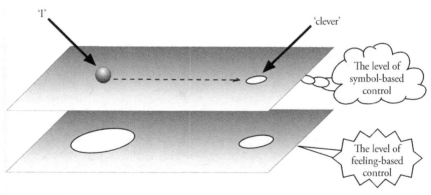

Figure 33

You must have noticed that the projection of the word 'clever' at the level of feeling-based control is shown as a white spot in Figure 33 because we attach a positive marker feeling to the word 'clever' just as we do to the word 'I'. What happens if I connect the word 'clever' to the word 'I'? This is shown in Figure 34.

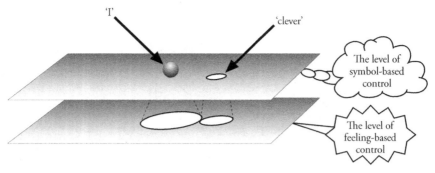

Figure 34

The large pool of positive marker feelings connected to the word 'I' at the level of feeling-based control is broadened with the positive marker feelings connected to the word 'clever' and, as a result, you will feel the strategic feeling of joy. What is the consequence of all this? That we try to connect the word 'clever' to the word 'I' in order to have a chance to experience the feeling of joy. (See Figure 35)

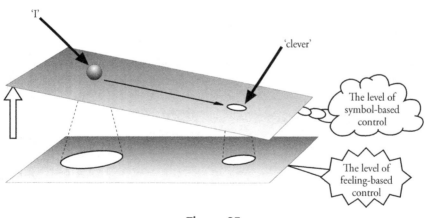

Figure 35

But in most cases, several words might appear as alternatives at the level of symbol-based control. (See Figure 36)

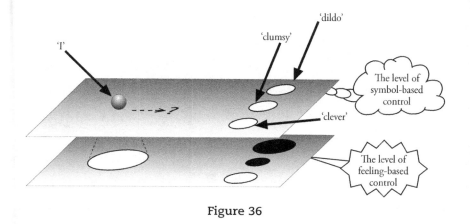

Figure 36

The processes taking place in Figure 36 are hard to interpret by only tilting the level of symbol-based control here and there, so we need to further develop our model. I suggest that we turn to Albert Einstein for help.

13.4.4 Curved space

Before Albert Einstein, physicists thought that space was a homogeneous and uniform something through which light travels in straight lines. But Einstein realised that large fields of gravity can bend space, so to speak, or deform it and that light does not travel in straight lines in this curved space. This phenomenon is often demonstrated with the simple experiment below. A rubber sheet is stretched out horizontally. In the first part of the experiment, a light ball representing a beam of light is rolled slowly on the rubber sheet. This ball travels in a straight line. This part of the experiment represents the physicists' theories from times before Einstein. (See Figure 37).

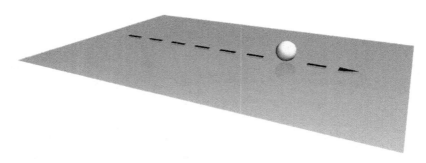

Figure 37

In the second part of the experiment, we put a heavy iron ball in the middle of the rubber sheet. This iron ball symbolises a high mass celestial body that has a strong field of gravity. We will see that the heavy iron ball pulls the rubber sheet down around it creating a gradually deepening funnel. Let us now roll the light ball again on the rubber sheet in a way that its path only slightly touches the edge of the funnel formed by the iron ball. If we roll the ball fast enough, we will see that the funnel slightly modifies the path of the ball. (See Figure 38)

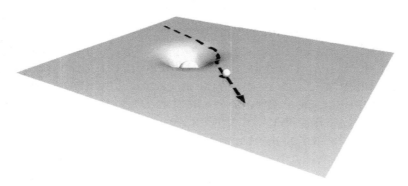

Figure 38

If the small ball is not fast enough, we will see that it rolls down in an ever-narrowing spiral to the bottom of the funnel formed by the heavy iron ball. The funnel here represents a black hole no beam of light can come out of.

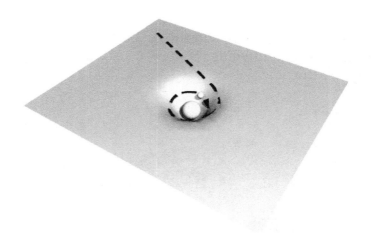

Figure 39

Well, the second part of the experiment represents Einstein's theory which symbolises how fields of gravity influence the way light travels. How is this experiment connected to human thinking? I guess some of you have now understood. The ideally stretched out rubber sheet in Figure 37 represents the ideas of the philosophers of ancient times about human thinking, whereas reality is shown in Figures 38 and 39. Yes, indeed. Our feelings bend and deform the space of human thinking. Marker feelings connected to certain words also divert our thinking in a similar way. There are some words whose marker feelings attract our thoughts and there are others that repulse them, as previously discussed.

I suggest now that we develop the experiment with the rubber sheet further. Imagine that negative marker feelings at the level of feeling-based control repulse, so to speak, the level of symbol-based control above them and deform it so that they form a little hump or hillock at the level of symbol-based control. Just as though we had trussed the rubber sheet with a stay-rod from below. (See Figure 40) The stronger the negative marker feelings connected to a given word are, the higher the hump will be. The positive marker feelings at the level of feeling-based control, in turn, attract the level of symbol-based control above and create holes in it as if we have put an iron ball on the rubber sheet. The stronger the positive marker feelings connected to a certain word are, the deeper the hole will be.

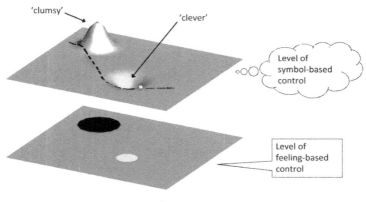

Figure 40

As a matter of fact, our thinking, like a small ball, rolls in a zigzag line among words defined by different marker feelings, i.e. around humps and holes of different heights and different depths, unlike the traditional theory that imagines human thinking as a linear, unbroken process. And see how much those tiny little marker feelings can influence our thinking and, together with it, also our fate.

An everyday example might be the following discussion between two girlfriends: "I'd like to introduce you to a very nice guy. He'd make an ideal husband. He's handsome, sporty and very muscular. He's a very good-humoured guy, he's nice and gentle and very understanding. And the biggest plus of all is that he likes doing housework. He cooks, he washes clothes and cleans the house. He's Mr Jackpot himself. He works in construction as a builder." "As a builder! Oh, c'mon. Forget it! I am going to marry a well-to-do doctor or a banker." And this way, she has perhaps ruined her life just because negative marker feelings were connected in her mind to the word 'builder'. In Figure 41, I show the processes taking place in the lady's mind.

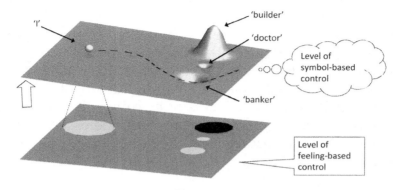

Figure 41

The white arrow on the left-hand side tilts the level of symbol-based control a little. This arrow symbolises one of the unpleasant need-indicating feelings of the need to reproduce, the motivational feeling of loneliness. The very strong negative marker feeling connected to the word 'builder' at the level of feeling-based control distorts the level of symbol-based control and forms a very high hump. The moderate positive marker feeling connected to the word 'doctor' at the level of feeling-based control also distorts the level of symbol-based control and forms a small hole. The stronger positive marker feeling connected to the word 'banker' at the level of feeling-based control distorts the level of symbol-based control and forms a larger hole.

What is the problem with this process? The lady does not make a decision on the basis of her feelings generated by her interactions with the external world but on the basis of a train of thought distorted by marker feelings connected to the imaginary world and therefore she becomes isolated from the external world. And as she made her decision in a different dimension, separated from the external world, she may have made the wrong decision. To put it more simply, instead of meeting the guy and making a decision on the basis of her feelings formed during the meeting, she is controlled by her prejudices.

But this is only one person's life. Carefully selected marker feelings can influence the lives of billions of people. That is why we do not call the defence industry the manslaughter machinery industry, that is why we call soldiers protectors and that is why we do not call them murderers. If we used different words, our fate would also be completely different. We would not serve as soldiers, and our bodies would not lie unrecognisably destroyed on the battlefields of faraway countries.

13.4.5 The use of marker feelings

Of course, my dear reader may ask why we need words with unpleasant feelings at all. Why can't we speak only with 'beautiful' words? Well, first of all, this is not a wishing game. The world is full of 'ugly' things and logically it is not possible, and it is not worth, describing them with 'beautiful' words. Second, marker feelings of different strengths and directions are connected to the same words in different people's minds. This is a question of education. There are layers of society where words like 'fuck' and 'whore', that have strong negative marker feelings for the average person, can be used without a problem. For these people, no negative marker feelings are connected to these words. And third, we need words which have negative marker feelings. For example in education. Words of different shades of marker feelings play an important role in the education not only of children, but also of adults. These feelings guide 'students' so they do not leave the right path. If they turn in the wrong direction, a word connected to negative marker feelings is attached to their name, which gives them a sign of warning or a 'mental slap in the face' that triggers more serious mental pain. If they behave appropriately, words connected to positive marker feelings are attached to their names, which triggers positive feelings. In other words, they are praised.

Okay, but sometimes even nice people use words that have negative marker feelings. Why do we call somebody a 'stupid prick'? The answer is simple. Because of anger. Anger is a strategic feeling which 'calls' us to behave aggressively against something or somebody. Sometimes this aggression only reaches the level of verbal aggression, where the goal is to cause mental pain to the other person. How can we do that? Well, definitely not by attaching words of nice and positive marker feelings to the name of the person under our attack. In order to hurt someone, we need to attach words of negative marker feelings to that person. And in that moment, a very interesting phenomenon takes place within us. The marker feelings connected to the level of symbol-based control get inverted, they turn to their opposite. Words of negative marker feelings will become attractive, and words of positive marker feelings will become repulsive for us. In other words, the humps in Figure 40 will become holes, and the holes will become humps. This lasts as long as our anger does. Then, the original status quo returns. Marker feelings connected to words do not change, but we select the words according to our current state of mind.

It is clear from the paragraphs above that strategic feelings such as desire, disgust, joy, mental pain, anger and love play an important role in the selection of words. This is only further modified and modulated by technological and status-indicating feelings. Of course, we must not forget about need-indicating and orienting feelings either because they generate strategic feelings to start with.

If, motivated by anger, we want to hurt someone, we can only do it with words of negative marker feelings. All that happens in such a case is that we 'hurt someone's ego' as they say. By the way, what is ego? Well, I could list millions of definitions from different books and lexicons that 'massage the air' in depth and talk about nothing. Nothing, because ego does not exist. The word 'ego' is nothing else but an imaginary word to which nothing but words can be assigned in the real world. The ego only exists in the form of words and by words. Don't you believe it? Try it. It doesn't cost a thing. Empty your mind and don't let any word appear there, then continue whatever you are doing: walk, do some gardening or cook. You will see that the 'ego' disappears. It is not there. But then, what gets hurt when somebody hurts us? Where and how do these processes take place?

At the level of feelings, of course. Because only feelings exist in our internal world. When we think, we do not just connect series of feelings of sounds, i.e. words, to one another, but also the feelings connected to those words. When we connect symbols, not only do we have to make sure that we map the world in the best possible way, but also that other feelings belonging to the symbols, words and series of feelings of sounds that we connect to one another also suit and match. In other words, our task is to connect feelings with other feelings without generating bad feelings in ourselves in the meantime. And this is where relational feelings (need-indicating, orienting, strategic and tactical feelings) and their concentrates and essences, i.e. marker feelings, have a decisive role. Relational feelings are connected to each and every word of the data network within us. These relational feelings are stronger for some words and weaker for others, sometimes they are positive, sometimes they are negative and sometimes they are neutral. While in dynamic speech and thinking these feelings become detached from words, their essences, marker feelings do not. They stay nicely stuck to the words and – just like relational feelings – they can also be stronger, weaker, positive, negative and neutral. When we assign two words to one another in the data network, not only do we connect the series of feelings of sound but also the groups of feelings belonging to them. What happens with the groups of feelings thus connected? They interact with one another. (See Figure 42)

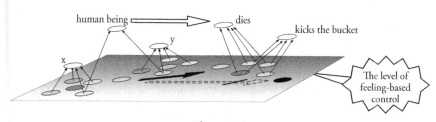

Figure 42

The lighter circles at the level of feeling-based control in Figure 42 symbolise feelings to which we attach the series of feelings of sound X and Y. X and Y do not represent imaginary words but specific persons. We arbitrarily select some of the feelings connected to X and Y and we assign the series of feelings of sound 'human being' to them. The word 'human being' is an imaginary word that is only slightly connected to the external world through the level of feeling-based control, i.e. it is only slightly anchored. The white circles on the right-hand side of the level of feeling-based control symbolise feelings to which we assign the series of feelings of sound 'dies' and 'kicks the bucket'. Both series of feelings of sound are connected to exactly the same feelings and phenomena. In simpler terms, they mean the same. Under each circle representing a particular series of feelings of sound, there are spots of different shades at the level of feeling-based control which symbolise the marker feelings connected to the given series of feelings of sound, as well as their quality and strength. Figure 42 shows that although in theory we could connect the series of feelings of sound 'human being' to both series of feelings of sound 'dies' and 'kicks the bucket' since they symbolise the same group of feelings or, in simpler terms, they mean the same, we still cannot do that because the very strong negative marker feeling connected to the phrase 'kicks the bucket' at the level of feeling-based control bans connecting the series of feelings of sound 'human being' and 'kicks the bucket'. By the way, I recommend that mathematicians dealing with the theory of networks pay attention to Figure 42 because this may be one of the starting points of modelling human thinking.

In the case of dynamic speech and thinking, primarily marker feelings interact with one another. They can weaken or strengthen each other. If we attach a word with a very strong negative marker feeling to a word with a very positive marker feeling, we seriously damage the positive marker feeling which triggers the feeling of mental pain. (See Figure 31). Attention! This applies to any word with positive marker feelings in our data network. This is important. So not only does it hurt when we attach a word with negative marker feelings to the symbol 'I' but also if I attach a word with negative marker feelings to any word with positive marker feelings. So if somebody swears at our mother, our home-land, our dog, our cat or our car, it will all hurt. Consequently, the series of feelings of sound 'I' – or as others call it with an undefined imaginary word: the 'ego' – is only one of the thousands of series of feelings of sound, or words, to which we attach positive marker feelings the destruction of which causes us pain.

"I don't get it." you could say "Why does it hurt someone if we destroy a positive marker feeling which is connected to a certain word in her mind?" The answer is in the controlling role of feelings. The strategic feeling of mental pain always stimulates us not to let somebody or something important to us get lost. How do we know that we are leaving a given interaction or a relationship? The intensity of the feelings typical of that relationship starts reducing. If these feelings are unpleasant, we feel relief, if they are pleasant, we experience the strategic feeling of mental pain which sends us the message not to let it go or get lost. And it is also true the other way round. When we are entering into a pleasant interaction, it manifests for us in the form of intensifying pleasant feelings. In these cases, another strategic feeling, the feeling of joy arises, which stimulates us to accept the given interaction.

Since, in practice, in dynamic speech and thinking, only marker feelings are connected to words and they play the dominant role, the strength of these marker feelings will give information about the status of a given relation, therefore we concentrate on the changes of marker feelings. We cannot do anything else because other feelings related to the words we are using are simply not present. The stronger the negative marker feeling a word connected to a word with a positive marker feeling has, the more we reduce the positive marker feeling and this reduction triggers the strategic feeling of mental pain which is in direct proportion to the reduction of the positive marker feeling. And the stronger the positive marker feeling a word connected to a word of positive marker feeling has, the greater the joy we will experience.

As a consequence, negative or positive marker feelings connected to neutral words trigger neither mental pain nor joy. Words with positive and negative marker feelings connected to words with negative marker feelings do not trigger particular types of strategic feelings, neither pain nor joy, anyway. It might happen that, controlled by the strategic feeling of anger, we could attach negative marker feelings in an attack of verbal aggression to words already having negative marker feelings, that is we swear at someone who we hate anyway but during this activity we only experience pleasant orienting feelings and not the strategic feeling of joy. To put it in simpler terms, we cannot be angry and joyful at the same time.

13.4.6 Marker feelings in our everyday life

And engineers and scientists have an advantage again. In their work, they can connect words of neutral marker feelings as they please. The only thing they need to pay attention to is that the data network they create properly describes the world. And what is the situation, for example, with scholars of theology? Oooooooh! They should only try to attach one single word that has even the slightest negative marker feeling to the word 'God'. But the same applies in general to philosophers and all other propagators of human studies. They need to be careful in selecting their words. For example, in Hungary there are no gypsies, only Roma. In the US, there are no Negroes, only Afro-Americans. Why? Because of marker feelings. The so-called pejorative words are all carriers of negative marker feelings.

Just imagine what would happen if a poor engineer was reprimanded by his boss: "What were you thinking of? How dare you call this part a 'cogwheel'? Do you have any idea what you have done?" "But I only wanted to find an apt name." "I don't care! From now on this part is called a 'knobwheel'. Did you understand? Otherwise you are fired." It would be really difficult to design an aeroplane like that. But this is exactly what happens in human studies. It does indeed matter what words they use. One occasion of using a careless – or as they say inappropriate – word and the person's career, or life, is done.

We may notice that as we move away from the level of physics, chemistry and biology, the role of marker feelings starts to increase. While it is very low at the level of the sciences, as mentioned above, their importance grows drastically in human studies. And it is completely natural! Of course, the words used in sciences have marker feelings but either their strength is very low or, in most cases, their sign is neutral and, as a consequence, they do not influence the flow of thoughts that much. On the other hand, in human studies, very strong marker feelings of decided signs are connected to the words people use. And these feelings do their job: they guide and control thoughts in silence. For example people for whom positive marker feelings are connected to the word 'democracy' will not readily enter into discussions about the advantages of dictatorship. They will avoid the use of the word 'dictatorship' in their thoughts exactly as if it were a vulgar swear word.

By the way, so many strong positive marker feelings are attached to the word democracy that it has become perfectly suitable for manipulating millions of people. It is enough to say there is no democracy in a given country, and thousands of people go to the streets immediately or spring to arms (arms are well-known instruments of democracy☺). And they do it without even being aware of the notion of democracy. They kill people or they sacrifice their life in the altar of an undefined imaginary word. When, why and how can people manipulate us with the word democracy? We need to look for the reasons in the economy. It is easiest to understand if we imagine the economy of our world as an enormous river in which there are strong currents under the surface. Individuals on the surface do not face the slightest chance to have an influence on the direction of the currents. They may try but it is in vain. That is if you try to change the direction of economic processes alone, you will be washed away by the current. So how can you influence the current? Actually, there are only two ways to do so. If you want to have an influence on those currents, either you need to create another strong economic current or you must try to modify the direction of the current with lots of people.

You can only achieve coordinated and unified actions of masses with central control. This can be done in various ways and you can also combine these ways. You can use a dictatorial system, you can use a system of uniform theories or you can use a combination of both as they did in the dictatorship of the proletariat. It does not make any difference for the masters of economic currents. And they do not care if it is done for a good or a bad purpose, the only thing that is important for them and that disturbs them is if people, controlled by a central will, step up in a uniform, coordinated and efficient way against the current of the river. How can the masters of economic currents protect themselves? It is simple. They need to destroy the unity. And suddenly the magician produces the word 'democracy' as he produces a rabbit out of a hat. And the intangible notion of democracy that means something different for everyone works miracles. The mass that was unified before breaks into pieces. What pieces? Who cares? The important thing is to get rid of their unity.

The most important achievement of today's world is democracy. Of course, we do not know where this undefined imaginary word comes from and what it means, but you can give it to the masses as a hobby horse to ride on. And while they are riding, they will not get organised. This is the achievement of Western democracies. And in the meantime, poverty increases all over the world, the middle classes of societies disappear and go bust and the gap between the destitute and the opulent becomes wider. But do not despair, you can be democratically destitute. Just imagine how bad it would feel to be well off in a dictatorial system (because there have been examples like that).

The masters of economic currents do not care about the fate of people as long as they do not block economic processes. Don't you believe it? Have a look at the countries of the Persian Gulf which definitely cannot be called democratic even if you are very lenient but since they have lots of oil, people do not block economic processes, so nobody cares the least if there is democracy there or not. Or let us have a look at African countries in poverty where people slaughter one another in bloody civil wars. Who cares? No one. Why? Because there are no significant economic interests they could hurt. Where are the heroic protectors of democracy in these cases where they are needed the most? The word 'democracy' is given very strong positive marker feelings, it is fetishized and declared to be more important than anything else and is set as a goal for people. This is what you call a scam.

The words democracy or dictatorship should not be goals for people, we should rather consider them as means. It would not make sense for soldiers to decide by voting whether they should spend their time drinking tea or making an assault on the enemy. But why could the inhabitants of a town not decide with a popular vote what kind of a theatre should be opened in their town. Strange as it may sound, mean things can be done under the auspices of democracy, and noble and humane things can also be done under the auspices of dictatorship exactly because these words symbolise the means and not the goal.

Needless to say, not everybody would be happy if somebody grounded the word 'democracy' or discarded it from the dictionary as a series of feelings of sound that does not mean anything because then you could not manipulate people with it any more. To clarify things, I do not have anything against the use of the series of feelings of sound 'democracy' but I think we should specify what it means beforehand and we should use it accordingly. (If my reasoning was too much to any of my readers, I suggest that you consult Figure 28)

Now that we have discussed the economy, let us have a look at the world advertisement. Although many people do not notice, the fight is furious there. Billions of dollars change hands (it is not about measly millions). What weapons are used in this fight? Naturally, the weapons of feelings. There are people who can only finance a handgun of feelings but some use heavy bombers. The fight is on for prestige. What is prestige? Prestige is nothing else but a very strong marker feeling connected to a given product, group of products or manufacturer. Just think about well-known manufacturers of perfumes or watches, designer companies or prestigious car brands. Do you think that a nice mass-produced wristwatch cannot show the time as accurately as a prestigious 'brand' product? Yes, they can. But it does make a difference what watch peeps out from under the sleeve of your jacket at a reception.

Because when you choose a watch you don't spend days consulting the technical documentation of watches. So it is not technical parameters but rather feelings, or more precisely, orienting feelings and marker feelings that you will base your decisions on. To put it more simply, you make a decision on the basis of aesthetics and prestige. Why do we choose prestige objects and clothes and why do we drive prestige cars? The answer is very simple: because these objects bestow the very strong positive marker feelings connected to them onto the person who is using them. The principal of expanding feelings is at work. They connect positive marker feelings to a given object with a well-designed advertisement campaign and the object, in turn, spreads the marker feelings connected to it to the person who is wearing or using it.

So what do we buy when we buy a posh watch? Primarily, we buy feelings and only secondarily do we buy a watch. We buy feelings because the watch will give us and our environment a positive marker feeling. We can look more important in other people's eyes by wearing a particular watch or jewellery or by driving a particular prestige car. Yes, clothes maketh the man. Or watches, or jewellery or a car. The more expensive, more refined and more prestigious the things you put on somebody, the greater a person he becomes! Although, it is not quite clear for me if we ornament a monkey with all these things, will it also become a great person?

And what is the case with scientific degrees and titles? Well, they are all carriers of strong marker feelings, what is more, they are explicit 'marker feeling billboards' and their job is exactly to connect the marker feeling of the appropriate strength to a given person. Why billboard? Because we rightly suppose that after obtaining a scientific title, the person will have the same mental capacities regardless of using or not using this title.

The situation is the same with soldiers. Different ranks are meant to declare different marker feelings. In the case of soldiers, however, we can use the notion of 'marker feeling billboards' literally as all the soldiers wear such billboards on their shoulders: their badges of rank. You can see from miles away what marker feelings you should attach to a particular person. Of course, it has some practical significance as well because a commander does not have to go to each and every soldier in the battlefield and shout his rank into their ears so they feel the appropriate marker feelings. Military decorations are also the carriers of marker feelings. And so are civilian awards as well. Although civilian awards are sometimes given just for fun, whereas soldiers give their blood for that little metallic badge.

And of course, we cannot leave out peerage titles either. Because peerage titles are naturally also 'marker feeling billboards'. Moreover, they are the non-plus ultra. Many-many people wanted, and still want, to add a nice chunky bit of a marker feeling, a peerage, to their names. The most ridiculous thing is that whereas in order to obtain other 'marker feeling billboards' you usually need to do something, peerages can be inherited. And they are inherited even if the offspring is a moral dwarf or – due to the intermarriages – a person of reduced mental abilities, a Sir 'Geoffrey Dumb'.

I remember when I was young and I was watching quiz shows or the elections on television, I was always puzzled to see how insignificant people get magical power in seconds. Let us take presidential elections for example. Often lesser-known politicians run as candidates for the position of the president of a country. Some of them people have already heard about but there are also some no one really knows. A common feature of these candidates is that they are usually 'second-line' politicians. Then the big day comes, and the results of the elections are announced. Television and radio channels broadcast the name of the winner at the same time. It takes one or two seconds for the speaker to announce the winner's name. What could possibly happen in those one or two seconds? Incredible things. The given person gets wings, as if he or she had collected more university degrees or more scientific titles in those one or two seconds.

But what does actually happen in those one or two seconds? What happens is we assign a title of incredibly strong marker feelings to a given person. This person becomes the president of a state, a religious leader, the chair of a political party, the winner of a song contest, the hero of the pub and so on. As a matter of fact, the principle of expanding feelings is also at work here. The positive marker feelings belonging to a given title are expanded to the person in question. And this procedure takes place in split seconds. An exception may be when we had negative marker feelings connected to the given person previously. This is when the war of marker feelings starts. And the outcome of the war depends on the strength of the marker feelings that participate in it.

And what is the situation with the truth? Unfortunately, truth is not unbiased either so the principle of expanding feelings works here as well. It does matter who tells you the truth. "A hick of a peasant took the courage to say that the Earth orbits around the Sun! What utter nonsense! His Excellency, Professor XY has long declared that it is the Sun that orbits around the Earth." Who would you believe if you were not aware of the laws of astrophysics? But people also use statements or quotes attributed to famous persons of unquestionable authority to prove different statements or opinions: Buddha, Jesus or Mohammed said… And that is the end of the dispute. It is finished, done, finito. Who dares to argue with people of such authority, the carriers of such strong positive marker feelings, or to question their statements?

We can only protect ourselves against marker feelings diverting our thoughts if we can have feedback from the world around us. That is why the representatives of the sciences have an advantage. People working in the sciences can have a little rest, can go back to 'reality', can build connections with the external world and can leave the level of symbol-based control and change to the level of feeling-based control. This is something the propagators of human studies cannot do. If a chemist says for example: "I'll go down to the lab and mix a bit of hydrogen sulphide." while she is uttering this sentence, she is at the level of symbol-based control and only marker feelings have an influence on her thoughts. Then she goes down to the laboratory and starts mixing things. While she is shaking her test tubes with her eyebrows pulled together, she interacts with the environment, incoming feelings flood her, she feels the piercing smell of hydrogen sulphide, in other words, she does not get separated from the external world. Thus, she has a chance to check the outcomes of her trains of thoughts and modify them, if necessary.

What is the situation with the propagators of human studies? When the philosopher says, for example, that: "I'll go to my study and think about the meaning of life." While he is uttering this sentence, his thoughts will be controlled by marker feelings similarly to the case of the chemist. But now comes the difference. While the chemist can leave the level of symbol-based control and can come across other feelings coming from the external world, the philosopher cannot leave the level of symbol-based control. If he wants to carry on thinking about the 'meaning of life', he will have to stay at the level of symbol-based control where his train of thought will be primarily influenced by marker feelings. This way, at least in terms of the subject of his thinking, he lives in an imaginary word isolated from the external world. He cannot directly check the appropriateness of his thinking since 'meaning' and 'life' are only words existing in his mind as series of feelings of sound. These things do not exist in the world around. His isolation from the external world can have detrimental consequences in terms of the outcome of his work. In the best case, he only builds castles of air that have nothing to do with the external world, but in the worst case, he tries to build these castles of air in the external world, sometimes ruining the lives of thousands or millions of people. (Not to mention that before thinking about 'the meaning of life' you should first clarify what is 'meaning' and 'life'.)

14.

THE BLACK HOLE

Although it is not the goal of this book to discover all the secrets of human thinking, there is a very important phenomenon I think we should spend a little time with. This is the phenomenon of black holes. As we mentioned previously, there are vast fields of gravity in the world of physics that soak up and –which is more important from our point of view – keep inside all materials including beams of light. Can we find a counterpart of the black hole phenomenon shown in Figure 39 in the field of human thinking? Can certain topics take our thoughts hostage? The answer to this question is a clear yes. Is it good or bad? Sometimes it is good, sometimes it is bad. It is bad if you are examining the 'Napoleons' of lunatic asylums or the members of extremist sects. It is good if you think of scientists who work persistently on a given topic, doctors who devote their energies to saving lives, or of composers or painters. And let us not forget about the obsessed thinkers, politicians or revolutionaries without whom humankind would be much poorer.

What made these people focus their thoughts on a given field? Naturally, it was their feelings. However, in order to understand how black holes are formed, it is not enough to examine the level of symbol-based control, i.e. the level of words or series of feelings of sound. We need to dig deeper. If I wanted to keep it short and simple, I could say an interplay of processes taking place at different levels of feelings is needed for the creation of black holes. I suggest that we start with a simple and easy-to-understand black hole which embitters our everyday life: the desire trap. Two things are necessary for the creation of a desire trap: desire itself and the fact that the subject of desire cannot be reached or obtained. This is perfectly understandable because if you already have the object of your desire, the feeling of desire itself disappears. For the sake of better understanding, I will try to demonstrate things with the help of diagrams.

Let us take as our starting point one of the need-indicating feelings of the need for energy supply: thirst. This unpleasant feeling can be shown as a hollow in a plane which, like it or not, you cannot get rid of. It keeps us hostage unless we meet the given need, that is unless we drink something. (See Figure 43)

Level of
need-indicating
feelings

Figure 43

There are cases, however, where we cannot meet a certain need immediately. In these cases, our memories from the past come back and we recall how we solved similar situations in the past. Based on our past experiences, words like 'beer' might appear at the level of symbol-based control. (See Figure 44)

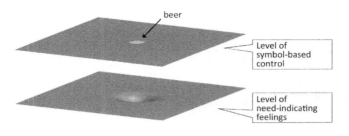

Figure 44

And then our memories related to drinking beer emerge from the past. We kind of feel them again and remember what beer drinking was like in the olden days. Although we are recalling memories from the past, as a matter of fact, we jump ahead into the future, we go time travelling and we give ourselves the experience of drinking a beer in advance, as if it had happened already.

Why is it important? Because during this imaginary beer drinking, we re-live feelings experienced during beer drinking. We see the glass sparkling with the foam on top of it, we feel how the cold and slightly bitter liquid floods our mouth. The pleasant orienting feelings experienced during beer drinking in the past come up. As a matter of fact, this takes place at several levels: as many levels as there are orienting feelings participating in the given process. But for the sake of keeping things simple, I will show them as one positive hump in one single level. (See Figure 45)

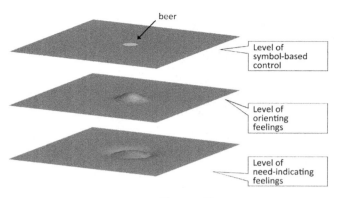

beer

Level of symbol-based control

Level of orienting feelings

Level of need-indicating feelings

Figure 45

You will notice a small change at the level of need-indicating feelings. After we recalled the pleasant orienting feelings connected to beer drinking from our memory, i.e. after we have focused our attention on the beer drinking in the future, the unpleasant need-indicating feeling reduces a little. (See Figure 45) As a matter of fact, it does not reduce, it's just that our attention is diverted from it and thus we feel its presence less.

However, due to the nature of things, we cannot always stay in the future, we need to come back to the present. And all the pleasant orienting feelings we were able to experience for a couple of moments now vanish into the thin air. The moment the pleasant orienting feelings disappear, the unpleasant strategic feeling of desire surfaces. And to make things even worse, our need-indicating feelings get a little stronger warning us that we are still thirsty and we should not stop drinking. I mean, imaginary drinking of course, because no real need satisfaction has taken place. (See Figure 46)

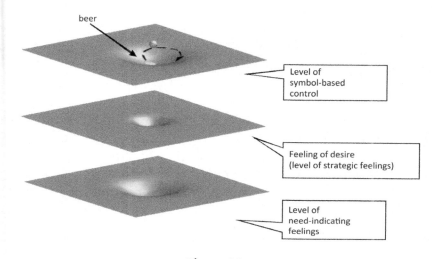

Figure 46

So we are in a worse position than before starting our time travel. Before we started, we had only experienced the unpleasant feeling of thirst but now that we have returned from the time travel, our thirst has intensified and is accompanied by the unpleasant strategic feeling of desire. How can we escape from our deteriorated situation? We cannot drink, so all we have left to do is travel in time again. And now we are entrapped. As a matter of fact, we do nothing else but jump back and forth between the stages shown in Figures 45 and 46 in a closed cycle (the only difference being that a new hollow is formed at the level of symbol-based control in Figure 45). And we simply cannot afford not to think of beer. All that happens is that the level of symbol-based control gets distorted by the levels below it. These levels distort space and a black hole, a thought trap, is created.

To the untrained eye, this is a thought trap, but we can now see that this situation is formed as a result of the interaction of different feelings and the main motivating force of the situation is the feeling of desire, so we can call this trap a desire trap. Naturally, this scenario does not only work with the word 'beer', it can work with anything you desire. The subject of your desire can also be 'Carol' but then different kinds of need-indicating and orienting feelings will participate in creating the trap. In this case, it will be the word 'Carol' we will not be able to get rid of. It is worth pointing out, however, that a desire trap is not yet love!

Since the formation of pleasant orienting feelings is enough to bring about desire, and the presence of need-indicating feelings is not a must, weaker desire traps can also be formed. For example, we can desire a bungalow, a yacht, a private jet or a luxury car one by one or altogether. In this case, our thoughts will be circling around the words 'bungalow', 'yacht', 'private jet' and 'luxury car'.

We can classify all the feeling traps – that is the desire trap, the tension trap, the fear trap, the game trap and the pain trap – as black holes or, in other words: thought traps. These feeling traps, although they primarily originate from the level of feelings of the traditional sense, naturally, the level of symbol-based control is also involved in the procedures of creating them. That is why it makes sense to name thought traps after the most important feelings participating in their formation.

An important criterion for the formation of black holes is that while we are thinking we need to give time for the feelings connected to the words to unfold. If we think in a fast and dynamic way, only marker feelings are present and the other feelings related to the words we are using do not have time to appear and therefore cannot influence us.

Why do scientists like to spend years thinking about a given issue? This must be terribly boring and tiring, you might think. What forces, or motivates, scientists to work on a given problem through years of terrible suffering and inhumane efforts? The answer is very simple. They do not suffer. What is more, they enjoy it. Those who like doing crosswords can easily understand a scientist. For scientists, their job is nothing but an endless and exciting crossword puzzle. What are the feelings that keep scientists within their field? The pleasant feelings scientists most often experience come from the group of orienting feelings. These orienting feelings are mostly acquired orienting feelings and can be connected to many things. They can be connected to the homely warmth of the laboratory, the soothing murmur of the equipment there, to the calmness or special smell of the room. Acquired orienting feelings can also connect to the process of thinking itself; to the creation of a nice and elegant train of thoughts, for example. In these cases, scientists do nothing but enjoy the beauty of the given train of thoughts. And this joy is actually nothing else but the experience of orienting feelings.

But we should not forget about strategic feelings either. There is desire that sometimes takes the form of curiosity and sometimes we simply desire to experience new pleasant orienting feelings. Or there is the feeling of joy. It is sometimes a storm of joy that wipes out everything and sometimes the small joys of everyday life that are given to us as presents after solving smaller parts of a problem. But the successes of scientists also help them satisfy the need of meeting others' expectations. When they are praised and celebrated for their achievements, they feel joy and pride. They can also satisfy the need of meeting their own expectations when they pat themselves on the back after the successful work. And, finally, they can also take steps ahead on the long path of self-realisation. That is why scientists concentrate on a given field of problems for years. If they tried to navigate to fields unknown for them, on the one hand they would risk being deprived of the pleasant feelings listed above and, on the other hand, they would also risk failures and loss of prestige in the unknown field. Pleasant present versus unpleasant future. That is why scientists' thoughts circle around a given problem sometimes for decades.

And last but not least, we need to deal with artificial back holes. Artificial black holes are deliberately created thought traps that keep people's thoughts concentrated on a particular subject. Traps created in this way are usually not autotelic. They almost exclusively serve the purpose of influencing and controlling the behaviour and activities of masses of people. Thought traps are tools that can be used for good and bad purposes, and in good or bad ways. They can make people's lives beautiful or miserable. The more a thought trap adapts to people's hierarchy of needs, the more comfortable and more liveable the given artificial thought trap is. And naturally, the opposite of this sentence is also true: the more a thought trap restricts people in meeting their needs, the more miserable it makes people's lives.

Since most of these systems have been developed to regulate people's behaviour, exactly because of their purpose, they actually make it impossible to achieve the top level of the needs hierarchy, i.e. self-realisation. There maybe one or two exceptions, systems that are not aimed at influencing people's behaviour but exactly at achieving a certain type of self-realisation.

Many feelings can participate in the creation of such thought traps but the most often used recipe is the combination of one of the indicating feelings of the need for security: fear, certain orienting feelings, the strategic feeling of joy, the technological feelings of tension and laxity, and déjà vu and status-indicating feelings. What are these artificial thought traps? I am not telling. This is a riddle. You'll have to solve it yourselves.

Naturally, just as you can create a thought trap for somebody else, you can also free yourself from one. Just like the way you can make 'antivirus programs' in information technology. If you can put these antivirus programs into somebody's mind, these programs will free the given person of thought traps and black holes and make the person immune to other viral thoughts as well.

15.

CONCLUSION

I think it is quite clear from what has been said so far that
- First, the method of thinking humankind uses most of the time, the method of thinking based on words, is full of inaccurately defined words.
- Second, this method is also full of errors due to changes of dimensions.
- And third, our feelings, in the traditional sense, influence our thinking in different ways and to different extents.

It is also quite clear that this is not a new phenomenon. It has been so since people living in the world learnt how to speak. Consequently, the knowledge base human-kind collected throughout its history is full of inaccurate words and definitions as well as errors due to changes of dimensions, diverted thoughts and distortions caused by feelings of the traditional sense. It is also clear that it is an unsustainable situation that has to be changed for the interest of humankind. How should we proceed?

Well, according to our current knowledge, humankind primarily uses symbol-based thinking to discover the world. We know two basic forms of this way of thinking: one form, which is readily available to everyone and is relatively easy to acquire, is traditional speech based on words, or series of feelings of sound. The other form, which is also readily available to everyone although it is harder to acquire, is mathematics that is also based on symbol-based thinking and the use of words, or series of feelings of sound. While speech has relatively flexible grammatical rules and many different kinds of feelings can be connected to individual words, mathematics has extremely strict 'grammatical rules' and is free of all kinds of feelings.

In speech, you have a chance to follow events taking place in the world but our feelings might divert our thoughts. In mathematics, our feelings of the traditional sense practically do not influence our thoughts, but mathematics does not always allow us to follow events taking place in the world because mathematics primarily takes its users to an imaginary world which sometimes does not have much to do with the external world. The outcomes of mathematical operations cannot be taken at face value because they might be flawless according to the rules of mathematics but still may have nothing to do with the world around us. Therefore, we always need to check the outcomes of mathematical operations and compare them to the external world (see the crazy tailor of Stanislaw Lem).

Why are people practising sciences successful? Because they use traditional thinking and mathematics together. As for the use of mathematical thinking in sciences, they always check the outcome of calculations in practice. And as for traditional speech, the words they use are relatively accurately defined, they use only a few imaginary words and even those are properly grounded, i.e. they are connected to the external world and relatively few feelings are connected to them.

So what is the secret of success? In what direction should human studies go? The answer is clear. It is in front of our eyes. We need to follow the proven and successful path of the sciences. There is no other way. The same key opens the door of the treasure house of the sciences and of human studies. In other words, the propagators of human studies must use accurately defined words, as few as possible imaginary words and if they need to use imaginary words, those imaginary words should be grounded and connected to the external world. They should also take into consideration the feelings connected to the words they use and their impact on their trains of thoughts. And they should not be afraid of mathematics! Yes, mathematics as a special, and in certain cases very effective, method of thinking does have a raison d'étre in the field of human studies as well.

Why do we need to do that? Because in the field of human studies, humankind is getting nowhere. In some fields – and these are the better cases – we stick with hundreds of years old theories and in other fields we stick with thousands of years old theories. It is not very likely, so to speak, that the forms of social organisation of today's world are the best possible. These forms need further development, and they can indeed be further developed with the appropriate means and knowledge. But just as the alchemists of olden days strove in vain to transform lead into gold without the appropriate knowledge base of nuclear physics, today's scientists are also striving in vain to create a better society, but while lacking the appropriate knowledge.

The number one task of our age is to lay the basis for, and develop, the science of feelings.

You may now think that this is just another piece of nonsense of mine and that it is much more important to give food to everyone so no one should starve in the world than exploring feelings. Well, as a matter of fact, humankind has been able to produce much more food than it could eat for a long time. There is only one reason why we haven't done so, and that is the form of our social organisation. People starve because of the backwardness of today's economy and the related political structures. In order to create a better society, however, we need to achieve a breakthrough in human studies. But that breakthrough is completely impossible without the lost 13th floor, without developing the science of feelings. Without it, we will only stumble from one economic crisis to another, from one war to another, we will exhaust the fossil and energy reserves of the planet, we will poison our environment and ruin the biosphere and all that waits for us is blood and despair. The sooner humankind realises the importance of the science of feelings, the less suffering we will face and the sooner we can start building a more developed societal structure.

However strange it may sound, it is psychology based on the science of feelings that must define the new basis of the science of economics. Psychologists have to find out what exactly we people need for a normal and humane life. And economists should implement the goals set for them. It would be a mistake to declare, on the basis of today's knowledge, that only the money-driven economic structures so typical of today's world are possible in the future. If, in the course of its development, humankind reaches a certain level, probably new opportunities will open in front of it. What kind of opportunities? Who knows? Just as the scientists of the olden days did not even dare to dream about the achievements of today's science, we cannot have accurate ideas about what achievements we may have and what new opportunities those achievements will open up. It is not our job anyway to daydream about the future. We must live in the present and solve the problems presented to us by our own age. So that for once our children, grandchildren and great-great-grandchildren can say that their ancestors did not live in vain because they laid the grounds for a better future.

16.

THINGS TO DO

I think no one questions how huge the task is. We need to change the way of thinking of all of humankind. Of course, we do not need to if we insist on maintaining the current situation. If you love mess, hopelessness, starvation, poverty and bloody wars, you definitely should not act. Then everything is good just as it is. But if you feel like living a more humane life, there is no other option than creating a more developed society. Theoretically speaking, there are two ways to do so. One of them is trial and error. This is nothing else than the automation of evolution: a species – in this particular case humankind – either survives or does not. Well, what if we do not succeed? Not much. Game over. (It is only a little extra that we cause suffering to billions of people.) The other way is if we try to use our brains while we are aware of the potential errors of our thinking. If we consider that we are human beings who exist through and by their feelings. Which way is the more humane and dignified? To march ahead towards the edge of the cliff or stand up on our feet and face the challenge?

No question: we need to lay down the scientific basis of a more developed society. I suggest setting up an International Humankind Research Institute, the acronym of which is

IHRI. Why international? The most important reason is to prevent power formations of individual countries from having an influence over the activities of the Institute. Because they will want to, that is for sure. A second reason why being international is important is because the achievements should be available for all the countries of the world. I mean, if the leaders of some countries do not curse the Institute and all its workers including the cleaner, the porter and even the porter's dog. Because there will be some who do. And third the financial background necessary for the operation of the institution can be provided more easily through international cooperation and it would mean less financial burden on individual countries. And if one or two financing countries withdraw, the Institute can still work.

Yes I know, by establishing this institute, less money can be spent on the production of stealth bombers, intercontinental missiles, nuclear submarines and other sophisticated killing machines but we will manage somehow. At least, I do hope so.

IHRI

What responsibilities would the IHRI have? It would be primarily responsible for working out, continuously developing, and correcting a society for humankind on a strictly scientific basis. What fields of research should be involved? Where should we start? On the 12th floor.
- A unit must be set up that would explore the mechanisms of feelings generated in human beings on the levels of neurobiology, biochemistry and biophysics.
- Another unit must be set up where the mechanisms of feelings generated in human beings, and the interactions of those feelings, are examined at the level of the science of feelings. In other words, we need to create a science of feelings.
And if we need to create it, we should give it an internation-

ally acceptable name. I would suggest matching the Latin for feeling 'sensus' and the Greek for science 'logos' creating the new word 'sensology' for our new science. This is going to be easy to adapt to other languages.

Coming back to the practical application of our new science, sensology, I would like to call the attention of the sensologists of the future to a very important phenomenon I was faced with after publishing my book *Feelings*. I saw that many people did not understand my book. They did not understand it because they were reading it as a dry mathematical treatise and they did not try to recall the feelings mentioned in my book, or in other words they only dealt with the issue on the level of symbol-based control. I hereby call to everybody's attention that you can only study feelings in a worthy way if you take the pain and find, explore and recall different feelings in yourself and you break up the third group of feelings originating from our internal world and examine their interactions. If you do not do that, it is exactly like writing a study about the famous painting of Leonardo da Vinci, *the Mona Lisa* without ever seeing the picture, or analysing Bach's *Toccata and Fugue in D minor* without ever listening to the piece and ever shivering when the organ starts. It is impossible to explore and understand the ocean of feelings at the level of symbol-based control: you need to immerse yourself in it. And you need to do it in a conscious way, paying attention to each and every detail.

- A unit must be set up to deal with the science of psychology. This unit will be responsible for developing the science of psychology using the achievements of the science of feelings.
- A unit must be set up where psychologists and sociologists examine how, and through which mechanisms, feelings generated in people modify feelings, and therefore the behaviour, of other people.
- A unit must be set up where psychologists, sociologists, linguists, economists, philosophers, historians, lawyers

225

and the scientists other human studies revise and reinterpret their fields of science.

"Why on earth should you reinterpret history?" Someone may ask. Because there are as many different histories as there are countries, ages, political and religious doctrines and economic interests. But the events happened only once and in one way! But of course, how could we understand the past, if we cannot even understand our present? Unfortunately today's history is nothing other than storytelling that serves the interests of those in power in a given country. So that is why history, and all other human studies, must be revised and reinterpreted. And it must be done on the basis of the achievements of the psychologists and sociologists of the previous unit. One of the results will be that a number of useless words will automatically be discarded whereas other, usable words will be grounded. This unit will be responsible for 'grounding' usable words. They will have to connect the usable words of their own fields of science to the external world. On the one hand, grounding words is a really easy task. All you need to do is describe how the processes symbolised by the given words work in the external world. On the other hand however, these processes are sometimes very difficult to explore.

Now that my dear readers have all the necessary knowledge, I suggest getting back to the definition of the word 'moral' mentioned in Chapter 10. How can we ground the word 'moral'? The definition of the word moral with imaginary words sounds like this: moral is the body of behavioural rules, collected by a society, which defines what is good and bad behaviour.

I think it is complete and easy to understand. We do not need a more accurate definition in our everyday life. However, we cannot be satisfied with this definition at the level of science. In order to give a more accurate definition, we need to examine how the notion of moral exists, and through which mechanisms it works, at the level of feelings. When we say someone is moral or immoral, we praise or reprimand the given person. This process takes place with the help of the very strong positive marker feeling connected to the word 'moral' and the very strong negative marker feeling connected to the word 'immoral' as we have seen in Chapter 13.4.5. As a consequence of the process above, the person we praised or reprimanded will experience mental pain or joy.

According to the rules of the levels of meeting others' expectations and meeting our own expectations, the person just praised or reprimanded will strive to experience as few unpleasant feelings as possible and as many pleasant feelings as possible. At the level of meetings others' expectations, you can achieve this if you try to avoid being reprimanded by others and try to deserve to be praised by others; at the level of meeting our own expectations, you can achieve this if you act in a way that you do not need to blame yourself for your behaviour and you trigger your own acknowledgement.

In this sense, moral is simply a collection of series of feelings of sound to which negative or positive marker feelings are connected. If you attach these series of feelings of sound to persons, they trigger positive and negative feelings in people, including the person they are attached to, thus regulating the behaviour of a person or persons.

But now I suggest getting back to the IHRI. The last unit in our list would be responsible for creating the list of defined words. The list of defined words will be practically a new and special monolingual dictionary in which only words that are grounded or connected to the external world could appear. And this unit will also be responsible for convincing scientists working in human studies to use only words appearing in the list of defined words in their works. Or if they still use an undefined word, it should be clearly differentiated from the rest of the text, for example they should italicise or underline it. I expect I've managed to upset some of you. "Who does this guy think he is? How dare he restrict the freedom of human thinking?" It is interesting that no one asks questions like this in the field of the sciences. If a physicist, a chemist or an engineer starts using undefined or unexplained words, they will simply think he is crazy and they will laugh at him. Imagine the following situation: "Dear colleagues! There is this double current, afterburner gas turbine. If we connect the stuff to the what's-its-name in the fuel tank, the thingy will stop fidgeting completely."

If somebody at home in the back garden tries to put together a flying object from suspicious parts collected from here and there, and she is fool enough to trust her life on this flying object, it is up to her. But when you need to create aeroplanes that carry hundreds of people, each and every part must be checked and thoroughly examined. The stamp of the technical controller must be butted in each and every piece together with the exact serial number.

But then, when we are laying the basis of a new social order based on scientific principles upon which the lives of billions of people will depend, can we just fabricate it from undefined words? We need to do exactly what is done in technical sciences. If somebody does not like the meaning of a word, he should explain why he does not agree with that particular definition and should recommend a new definition.

The issue of defining words causes problems also in other fields. We often come across serious legal documents where a complete chapter is given to the definition and interpretation of important terms and expressions. And this is a well-established practice. Why couldn't we do the same in the field of human studies? But of course with much higher accuracy. Humankind will also have to choose a base language the grounded words of which would serve as an example for all languages. I think English would be most suitable candidate on the one hand because of its immense vocabulary, and on the other hand because of its widespread nature.

– A unit will must be set up where the achievements of different fields of the arts will be revised, classified according to new criteria and assessed.

"Why on earth would you need to revise the arts?" you may ask. Because a work of art is nothing else but a transformation of the external world controlled by the specific feelings of the creator and aimed at triggering specific feelings in people. This is the grounded definition of 'work of art'. How can you assess or understand a work of art without studying and understanding feelings? No way. If you want to understand a work of art, you need to examine what feelings the person who ordered the given work of art, the artist and the people who enjoyed the given work of art experienced in different historical ages.

By the way, if we are already talking about art, I suggest that we get back to the issue of grounding the notion of beauty, as I promised in Chapter 13.4.1. We denote pleasant orienting feelings generated during seeing and hearing with the word 'beauty'. In other words, because something is beautiful, that thing generates pleasant orienting feelings in us. Similarly, we denote pleasant orienting feelings arising in us while eating food with the word 'fine'. By grounding and defining 'work of art' and 'beauty' we not only say farewell to a number of misconceptions, but we also open up new prospects for the creation of scientifically based works of art. (I know these sentences have made many of you writhe but please consult Figure 28)

And of course a unit must be set up that would create – taking into consideration everything that has been said so far – the system of criteria a scientifically based society must meet at the level of feelings. In other words they will define what people need in order to live a happy life. This is a very important question because **this is the goal itself!** We need to ask the question of what an ideal society would be like if all the circumstances were perfect granted during its creation. And it is not enough to ask the question, we also need to answer it... And the answer is the ideal goal itself to which we need to get as close as possible in practice.

And now dear members of the world (shadow) government – if such a thing exists at all – dear multibillionaires! While you definitely have much more information than people living at other levels of society, from your heights even you cannot see the way out from humankind's current situation. You cannot see it because no one has found it yet and no one will if we do not put things in order in the field of human studies. It is your responsibility to provide the prerequisites for the search for the right way. This is not the responsibility of uneducated people living in need and poverty.

You know that leadership is not about privileges but responsibility. Currently you are primarily concerned with obtaining and keeping privileges. One thing, however, escapes your attention and it is the fact that we are all living in the same society. Your welfare can survive the decline, or potential fall, of the society only for a short time. Your welfare comes from the society from which you feed through your roots. The worse the soil, the more incomplete the plants which grow in it. So you should pay some attention to the soil.

Now you can still move from one country to another if the soil becomes exhausted in one place, or you can spread your roots throughout the world but eventually you will share the fate of the rest of the world's population. If the future of humankind is the edge of the cliff, the same edge of the cliff is waiting for you too. This is something you should not forget. When you are governed by responsibility felt for the fate of other people, you are also acting for your own successors. What are you waiting for? What can you lose? What would you lose if you supported the establishment of such an institute? Now you have the chance to show you are worth something, you can do something for humankind and you did not live a pointless life on Earth. Make people remember you. Do not be like the long forgotten aristocrats of past times because no one remembers them anymore. Act so that your grandchildren and great-grandchildren can say my ancestor did something for humanity. Is it not worth doing something for such a goal? If not, then what is worth it?

- And of course, a unit must be set up that examines the feasibility of the ideal goal in practice.

And this is going to be tough. Even tougher than the others. Although the operation of the entire Institute will rub people up the wrong way, this unit will definitely be the last straw. Because while strange guys are thinking about inconceivable things in a closed Institute, it does not really concern others. But if they try to bring these things out from the Institute and implement them in everyday life, this is where things will break loose. So it makes sense to classify the current operation of the Institute. I mean, classify the process, not the results. External social forces must not have an influence on the research taking place in the Institute. Within the Institute, however, absolutely free thinking must be ensured for, and be required from, its employees. Because our world is full of obvious things which, although they are true, they must not be talked about. For example you must not talk about....... Or you would rather avoid talking about....... Not to mention the issue of........ Why did I not write the words? You definitely do not expect me to risk the success of my book or risk being excommunicated or even risk my life or my family's lives. Think! Replace the dotted lines with words for yourselves. You will find a great many words, I can assure you.

Why is it important? Imagine the following discussion in an institute of aeroplane design: "What are you thinking, you idiot! I have told you not to deal with the issue of engines. How many times do I need to repeat it? You can deal with the colour of the pilot's seat or how many rolls of toilet paper can be placed in the restroom but forget the word 'engine' for ever!" Well, my dear reader, do you think the aeroplane could ever take off without an engine? No way. Can we create the science-based society of the future without discussing the hardest issues? Never, ever. That is why we need to explore and discuss the most sensitive issues the most. And in order to do so, we need to ensure the appropriate conditions so that no one ever can terrorise the employees of the Institute because of their thoughts.

– And of course, we will need another unit for checking the results.

The other day I was trying to put my books in order, and I bumped into a tattered old book with pages turned yellow. The book was written in 1942. I read it when I was about 10 and I found it very intriguing. The book was written by Isaac Asimov and the title was *Foundation*. The book was about a group of scientists, mathematicians trying to save the inhabitants of the Galaxy from 30,000 years of pointless suffering with the help of a new science, a kind of a mixture between statistics and probability theory. They do it by creating, with the help of psychologists, a mathematical tool which makes it possible to model the behaviour of a group of people above a critical mass with high probability. Well, my dear readers, I think the time has come when we can turn this book from science fiction into science.

Yes, the time has really come, and we can create a mathematical model that is capable of modelling the behaviour of larger groups of people. But there is a prerequisite and this is the science of feelings. Because without the science of feelings, it will not work. This is where I would like to call the attention of researchers in the field of artificial intelligence to the fact that although your research might be successful in certain respects, if you try to model human thinking without paying attention to feelings, you are prone to failure. Today, we cannot describe and model individual behaviour at the level of nerve cells, but we could do it at the level of feelings. It is more a question of commitment and money. Of course it is not really worth modelling personal behaviour except if the given person is in a very important position. The analysis of the behaviour of larger groups of people, however, is a much more exciting issue.

Well, the given unit, apart from creating the mathematical apparatus, will also be responsible for checking and modelling the results of the different units before implementing them in a large-scale live environment.

– Then we will also need a communications unit.

With a very well prepared and cunning staff. They will be responsible for presenting the results of the Institute to the public in a digestible form. Why is it a sensitive and complicated task? Because you cannot just replace the supporting pillars of people's thinking the way you replace the operating system of your computer. When you replace the operating system, you need to switch off and restart your computer. You cannot switch off and restart people. Or, to be more precise, you can switch them off as has been proven by the history of humankind, as many idiot oppressors got as far as switching people off, i.e. killing them and massacring them, but somehow they forgot about the restart.

Why did they have to do away with so many people? Because they could not change their thinking. If they could have reprogrammed them simply by pushing a button, they could have lived on. You know the saying: "If you get rid of the person, you get rid of the problem." This saying is well-established practice even today. Well, this unit would be responsible for transforming the supporting pillars of the thinking of humankind step-by-step. Attention! I am not talking about organising a 'thought police'. You only need to transform the basis and guide people in the right direction.

This unit would be responsible for example for working out the curriculum and syllabus of the school subject 'sensology' and the related exercises. This is where we need to lay great emphasis on drills and practice. Because if you do not do so, it would be like the person who learned how to play the piano in theory. Education must be started in childhood so that the things we, the older generations can only understand with great difficulty, would be easy and straightforward to our sons and daughters. The introduction of the school subject 'sensology' will have an enormous social significance. A new type of very sensitive and conscious people will start to appear, there will be more and more of them and eventually they will rule society. And the grounded words will do the job in silence: chaos will disappear and a crystal clear and transparent world will emerge. This will result in a quantum leap and will open new dimensions for humankind. Do not forget, however, that a prerequisite of this is the exploration of the world of feelings and the development of the science of feelings, sensology.

My dear reader, we have come to the end of my book. The goal is set and you know what to do. I hope fate will be gracious to us people, and we will have the chance to start walking on the right path.